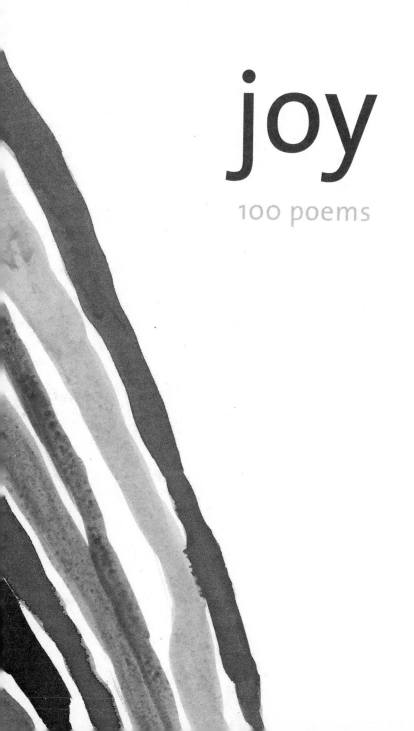

edited by christian wiman

joy

100 poems

Yale University Press books may be purchased in quantity for educational, business, or promotional use. For information, please e-mail sales.press@ yale.edu (U.S. office) or sales@yaleup.co.uk (U.K. office).

Designed by NANCY OVEDOVITZ and set in The Sans and Sabon type by INTEGRATED PUBLISHING SOLUTIONS, GRAND RAPIDS, MICHIGAN. Printed in the United States of America.

Library of Congress Control Number: 2017934780
ISBN 978-0-300-22608-9 (hardcover : alk. paper)

A catalogue record for this book is available from the British Library.

This paper meets the requirements of ANSI/NISO Z39.481-992 (Permanence of Paper).

10 9 8 7 6 5 4 3 2 1

CONTENTS

Still Wilderness CHRISTIAN WIMAN xi

A Note on the Selections xxxviii

First Song GALWAY KINNELL 3

from The Precision of Pain and the Blurriness of Joy: The Touch of
Longing Is Everywhere YEHUDA AMICHAI (translated from the
Hebrew by Chana Bloch and Chana Kronfeld) 4

Canal Bank Walk PATRICK KAVANAGH 5

This Is Us Saint's Day JEN HADFIELD 7

Travelin' Shoes CORNELIUS EADY 8

The Blessing of the Old Woman, the Tulip, and the Dog
ALICIA SUSKIN OSTRIKER 9

Hamlen Brook RICHARD WILBUR 11

hag riding LUCILLE CLIFTON 12

Small Moth SARAH LINDSAY 13

And We Love Life MAHMOUD DARWISH (translated from the Arabic by Fady
Joudah) 14

To Make a Summer JOSEPHINE MILES 15

The Crowd CHARLES BAUDELAIRE (translated from the French by Keith
Waldrop) 16

The Dancing GERALD STERN 17

With wine and being lost, with PAUL CELAN (translated from the German by
Nikolai Popov and Heather McHugh) 18

Out at Lanesville DAVID FERRY 20

The Bluet JAMES SCHUYLER 23

Hip-Hop Ghazal PATRICIA SMITH 25

Temptation NINA CASSIAN (translated from the Romanian by Brenda Walker and Andrea Deletant) 26

Loony-Bin Basketball MARY KARR 27

Pastoral RITA DOVE 29

Waking with Russell DON PATERSON 30

You're SYLVIA PLATH 31

Danse Russe WILLIAM CARLOS WILLIAMS 33

Summer Kitchen DONALD HALL 34

The Second Madrigal ANNA SWIR (translated from the Polish by Czesław Miłosz and Leonard Nathan) 35

A Brief for the Defense JACK GILBERT 36

Tea at the Palaz of Hoon WALLACE STEVENS 37

Susie Asado GERTRUDE STEIN 38

Joy LISEL MUELLER 40

the rites for Cousin Vit GWENDOLYN BROOKS 41

One of the Many Days NORMAN MACCAIG 42

The Moose ELIZABETH BISHOP 44

Best Laid MAUREEN N. MCLANE 51

Deaf Mute in the Pear Tree P. K. PAGE 52

From Blossoms LI-YOUNG LEE 54

"Who never wanted—maddest Joy" EMILY DICKINSON 56

Hurrahing in Harvest GERARD MANLEY HOPKINS 57

Laundromat LORINE NIEDECKER 58

Late Beethoven ADAM ZAGAJEWSKI (translated from the Polish by Renata Gorczyńska) 59

The Ninth Symphony of Beethoven Understood at Last as a Sexual
    Message ADRIENNE RICH 62

Big Finish KIMBERLY JOHNSON 63

Unrelenting Flood WILLIAM MATTHEWS 64

Meditation on a Grapefruit CRAIG ARNOLD 66

Blackbird Étude A. E. STALLINGS 69

Slim in Atlanta STERLING A. BROWN 70

Station MARIA HUMMEL 73

A Poem for the Epiphany PABLO MEDINA (translated from the Spanish by
    the author) 74

Often I Am Permitted to Return to a Meadow ROBERT DUNCAN 77

Wedding Poem ROSS GAY 80

Once in a Lifetime, Snow LES MURRAY 82

Pentecost MICHAEL DONAGHY 85

C Major TOMAS TRANSTRÖMER (translated from the Swedish by
    Robin Fulton) 86

to the sea ARACELIS GIRMAY 87

Plumbing RUTH STONE 89

The Joy of Writing WISŁAWA SZYMBORSKA (translated from the Polish by
    Clare Cavanagh and Stanisław Barańczak) 91

Meeting Point LOUIS MACNEICE 93

Coming HEATHER MCHUGH 95

True Love SHARON OLDS 98

Once, I JANE HIRSHFIELD 99

Tractor TED HUGHES 100

Yoko THOM GUNN 104

from Vacillation W. B. YEATS 107

Memoir VIJAY SESHADRI 108

The Rapture of Dry Ice Burning Off Skin as the Moment of the Soul's
Apotheosis THYLIAS MOSS 109

And I Was Alive OSIP MANDELSTAM (translated from the Russian by
Christian Wiman) 112

Little Clown, My Heart SANDRA CISNEROS 115

Land's End AUGUST KLEINZAHLER 116

Procedure JO SHAPCOTT 119

Ode to the Urge RICARDO CASTILLO (translated from the Spanish by
Robert L. Jones) 120

Lore R. S. THOMAS 121

from Poems for Moscow MARINA TSVETAEVA (translated from the
Russian by Ilya Kaminsky and Jean Valentine) 122

The Season of Phantasmal Peace DEREK WALCOTT 123

But I, too, want to be a poet FANNY HOWE 125

Dawn Outside the City Walls JUAN RAMÓN JIMÉNEZ (translated from
the Spanish by Robert Bly) 127

The Ache of Marriage DENISE LEVERTOV 128

Happiness PAISLEY REKDAL 130

Accidents of Birth WILLIAM MEREDITH 132

Far from Kingdoms PATRIZIA CAVALLI (translated from the Italian by
Judith Baumel) 134

I'd Rather Go with You DANIELLE CHAPMAN 135

Coming PHILIP LARKIN 136

King David Dances JOHN BERRYMAN 138

The Answer SARA TEASDALE 139

Epitaph H.D. 140

The Lemons EUGENIO MONTALE (translated from the Italian by
    Jonathan Galassi) 141

Manifesto: The Mad Farmer Liberation Front WENDELL BERRY 144

"Love of My Flesh, Living Death" LORNA DEE CERVANTES 146

Glamourie KATHLEEN JAMIE 148

After Arguing against the Contention That Art Must Come from
    Discontent WILLIAM STAFFORD 150

Half a Double Sonnet MARY JO SALTER 152

Warning TAHA MUHAMMAD ALI (translated from the Arabic by Peter Cole,
    Yahya Hijazi, and Gabriel Levin) 153

Directive ROBERT FROST 154

Old Pewter SEAMUS HEANEY 157

Well Water RANDALL JARRELL 160

Here GRACE PALEY 162

Joy ROBINSON JEFFERS 164

What Are Years MARIANNE MOORE 165

Yes MURIEL RUKEYSER 166

Ideal Audience KAY RYAN 169

The City Limits A. R. AMMONS 171

An Old Cracked Tune STANLEY KUNITZ 173

Acknowledgments 175

Credits 176

STILL WILDERNESS

I.

Paul Tillich once said of the word "faith" that "it belongs to those terms which need healing before they can be used for the healing of men." The word "joy" may not be quite so wounded, though I have noticed, as I have mentioned this project to people over the past year, that it does provoke some conflicting responses. There is the backslapping bonhomie of the evangelically joyful, who smile as if to say, "Even you, Old Sludge, dire poet—of our party at last!" There is academic detachment: Is joy merely an intensification of happiness or an altogether other order of experience? And is it something of which one can be conscious at all, or is it so defined by immersion in a present tense that consciousness as we conceive it is precluded? There is affront: ruined migrants spilling over borders, rabid politicians frothing for power, terrorists detonating their own insides like terrible literal metaphors for an entire time gone wrong—"How with this rage shall beauty hold a plea," as Shakespeare, staring down his own age's accelerating grimace, wondered. I took on this project because I realized that I was somewhat confused about the word myself, and I have found that, for me, the best way of thinking through any existential problem is with poetry, which does not "think through" such a problem so much as undergo it. Subjected to poetry's extremities of form and feeling, what might that one word, in these wild times, mean?

Here is the definition of "joy" from Merriam-Webster:

1: the emotion evoked by well-being, success, or good fortune or by the prospect of possessing what one desires
2: a state of happiness or felicity: bliss
3: a source or cause of delight

If you're musing on the general meaning of joy or sitting down to write an article on the subject, this might be of some use as a place to start. But if you are trying to understand why a moment of joy can blast you right out of the life to which it makes you all the more lovingly and tenaciously attached, or why this lift into pure bliss might also entail a steep drop of concomitant loss, or how in the midst of great grief some fugitive and inexplicable joy might, like one tiny flower in a land of ash, bloom—well, in these cases the dictionary is useless.

Here is an alternative:

One of the Many Days
I never saw more frogs
than once at the back of Ben Dorain.
Joseph-coated, they ambled and jumped
in the sweet marsh grass
like coloured ideas.

The river ran glass in the sun.
I waded in the jocular water
of Loch Lyon. A parcel of hinds
gave the V-sign with their ears, then
ran off and off till they were
cantering crumbs. I watched *whimsy*
a whole long day
release its miracles.

But clearest of all I remember
the Joseph-coated frogs
amiably ambling or
jumping into the air—like
coloured ideas

tinily considering   7
the huge concept of Ben Dorain.

NORMAN MACCAIG

It is a real pleasure to ponder the small stops of kinetic clarity this poem manages. The river *ran glass* in the sun. *Jocular water.* The *cantering crumbs* that the hinds become in a distance that is both literal and lost, observed and remembered. And of course there are those *Joseph-coated* frogs, which don't leap out of the actual into the mythological but bring the myth smack-dab into matter. Thus "One of the Many Days" names and consecrates all of the days, even as it gives form and pledges fidelity to a single one. And just as the frogs are probably not really "considering" the concept of Ben Dorain, so the poet perhaps—and all of us along for the ride with him—stands in relation to some larger reality that this poem at once implies and denies: yes, there is that word "miracles," but it is obvious that they have no existence apart from the actual. These metaphysical resonances are not added to the poem but implicit within it. God is a ghost only to those who haunt their own lives, the poem might be saying. Or: God is a given for those who fully inhabit their own lives ("a joy/in which faith is self-evident," as Adam Zagajewski says). The word "God" is both inevitable and extraneous to this poem, as is the word "joy." "One of the Many Days" describes a moment of consciousness in which, as MacCaig puts it in another poem:

> Space opens and from the heart of the matter
> sheds a descending grace that makes
> for a moment, that naked thing, Being,
> a thing to understand.

2.

"Joy is the present tense, with the whole emphasis on the *present*," writes Kierkegaard. This is accurate insofar as it accords with the feeling of joy, which can banish all the retrospective and anticipatory mental noise we move through most of the time. But to define joy as present tense is to keep it fastened to time, and that doesn't feel completely right. It might be truer to say that joy is a flash of eternity that *illuminates* time, but the word "eternity" does sit a bit lumpishly there on the page. Let's try this:

Small Moth
She's slicing ripe white peaches
into the Tony the Tiger bowl
and dropping slivers for the dog
poised vibrating by her foot to stop their fall
when she spots it, camouflaged,
a glimmer and then full on—
happiness, plashing blunt soft wings
inside her as if it wants
to escape again.

Here is another poem in which joy is not mentioned, but I would argue that it is a moment of joy that has enabled Sarah Lindsay to see her happiness. What is the difference? For now, let the poem be the guide. Something intimately related to time but ultimately beyond it, something as remote and inconceivable as a comprehensive awareness of one's entire life, and yet as near and ordinary as a small moth, has broken into and illuminated—and perhaps even suggested the final fruition of?—time. Note just how much work that one word "plashing" is doing in this scrupulously plainspoken poem. It is as if the moth has entered from another element, or has momentarily transformed the element into which it has come, where everything is so slow and singularly itself it seems to be suspended in water.

3.

A moment of insight, then, a spot of time, in William Wordsworth's language—and indeed Wordsworth is the great English poet of joy. MacCaig's four lines (and most of this book) have their origins in a famous passage from "Tintern Abbey," which Wordsworth wrote after returning as a young man to a landscape of his childhood:

> These beauteous forms,
> Through a long absence, have not been to me
> As is a landscape to a blind man's eye:
> But oft, in lonely rooms, and 'mid the din
> Of towns and cities, I have owed to them,
> In hours of weariness, sensations sweet,
> Felt in the blood, and felt along the heart;
> And passing even into my purer mind
> With tranquil restoration:—feelings too
> Of unremembered pleasure: such, perhaps,
> As have no slight or trivial influence
> On that best portion of a good man's life,
> His little, nameless, unremembered, acts
> Of kindness and of love. Nor less, I trust,
> To them I may have owed another gift,
> Of aspect more sublime; that blessed mood,
> In which the burthen of the mystery,
> In which the heavy and the weary weight

Of all this unintelligible world,
Is lightened:—that serene and blessed mood,
In which the affections gently lead us on,—
Until, the breath of this corporeal frame
And even the motion of our human blood
Almost suspended, we are laid asleep
In body, and become a living soul:
While with an eye made quiet by the power
Of harmony, and the deep power of joy,
We see into the life of things.

Precision in poetry happens in different ways. The most obvious is imagistic, like that "vibrating" dog in Lindsay's poem (or like most of the scene-setting that precedes the passage I have quoted from "Tintern Abbey"). Language drapes the world like dew and sharply clarifies a scene that, inevitably, it only glosses. There are vast differences of degree here, from simple description to blazing revelation, but the emphasis is on the eye. Sometimes, though, when the poet's ear is as finely tuned as her eye, the words can seem to penetrate the world at which they are aimed—MacCaig's "jocular water," for instance, the fluent crispness of which conjures the river it describes, or Lindsay's "blunt, soft wings" which are themselves monosyllabic wing beats. And then sometimes, as with music, a poem can acquire a formal dynamism that is much greater than its parts, an almost metaphysical precision, in which the sonic currents don't merely imitate but seem to participate in the very existence of what they describe. Seamus Heaney has pointed out the effect of panoramic suspension combined with exacting particularity that one gets from Wordsworth's poetry (especially *The Prelude*). I would take it one step further. The eye is suspended over the earth, but the ear is immersed within it, as if the poet were hovering over what he is also inside.

Form matches theme here. The passage above is in many ways a classical depiction of a moment of joy, yet Wordsworth is careful to make joy only one of the catalysts. The other component, according to Wordsworth, is the awesome formal harmony of nature, which has made the speaker quiet, receptive, and *able* to see into the life of things. True vision, the poem says, is reciprocal: the world looks back at the eye that is strong enough (fortified by memory, alert to goodness) and weak enough (made quiet, the ego not eradicated but refined) to see it.

And why shouldn't this be so? There is a connection, after all, between the life of things and human life. We are both, quite literally, resurrected stars, compacted of the same random atoms, and we now know for a fact what in 1798 Wordsworth was only intuiting: some particles are so intimately related that they cannot be described independently and can communicate (are "entangled") over apparently limitless distances of space and time. It is a great mystery—and at times a great horror—to ponder the link between man and matter, the intimacies that our visions reveal, and that our daily lives so routinely violate. "Are we to think," asks Jacques Maritain, "that in such an experience, creative in nature, Things are grasped in the Self and the Self is grasped in Things, and subjectivity becomes a means of catching obscurely the inner side of things?" Reading Wordsworth, I would say yes.

4.

The definition of joy in the passage by Wordsworth and Mac-Caig, though tethered tightly to the natural world, remains pretty abstract. Even "Small Moth," clear as it is on the elements of one woman's happiness, is elusive about that moment of joy. This may be inevitable, though this entire book is aimed against whatever glitch in us or whim of God has made our most transcendent moments resistant to description. ("A revenge of a mortal hand," is how Wisława Szymborska defines the joy of writing.) The great Israeli poet Yehuda Amichai once wondered why it is that we have such various and discriminating language for our pains but become such hapless generalizers for our joys. "I want to describe," his poem concludes, "with a sharp pain's precision, happiness / and blurry joy. I learned to speak among the pains."

"Among the pains" is where we all learned to speak. The instant the link between word and world appears, so does the rift between them. (I met a Czech scholar once, a man of immense learning and multiple languages, who told me that he didn't speak a word until he was five years old. "Everything was okay until then," he said with a shrug.) This link/loss aspect of speech seems true no matter one's metaphysical dispensations. You don't need to believe that the meaning of the word "love"—or even, say, "rock"— has been plumbed in order to maintain that language has not exhausted it.

Still, as I have been suggesting, joy is quite particular in its resistance to particularity. What is it we are feeling when we are feeling joy? In Lisel Mueller's poem "Joy" someone breaks into tears upon hearing a passage of beautiful music:

It's only music. And it was only spring,
the world's unreasoning body
run amok, like a saint's, with glory,

that overwhelmed a young girl
into unreasoning sadness.
"Crazy," she told herself,
"I should be dancing with happiness."

But it happened again. It happens
when we make bottomless love—
there follows a bottomless sadness
which is not despair
but its nameless opposite.
It has nothing to do with the passing of time.
It's not about loss. It's about
two seemingly parallel lines
suddenly coming together
inside us, in some place
that is still wilderness.

Still wilderness. The place that is most us yet remains beyond us.
("You are in me deeper than I am in me," says Augustine of God.)
The particles of burned-out stars that are, or are trying to be, still
on fire. ("You'll feel light gliding across the cornea / like the train of
a dress," says Nina Cassian.) All this intimate and alien energy, all
this rejuvenating and ravening matter, stilled.

5.

And now what, one might fairly ask? After one has seen into the life
of things, after the moment that is still wilderness has evaporated
into the demanding and utterly domestic next, after one has looked
up from the tiny miraculous moth to find oneself right back in plain
old Tony-the-Tiger time—now what?

Pain, for one thing:

> Joy's trick is to supply
> Dry lips with what can cool and slake,
> Leaving them dumbstruck also with an ache
> Nothing can satisfy.

RICHARD WILBUR

But this is a special kind of pain. ("It's not about loss," as Mueller says.) It is a homesickness for a home you were not aware of having. A longing you hardly knew you had has been both answered and, because now there is nothing you want more than to have, not this experience again exactly, but the larger one that it let you glimpse, intensified. But there's no forcing it. Clamoring after joy leads only to fevered simulacra: an art of professional echoes and planned epiphanies, the collective swells of manipulative religion, the manufactured euphoria of drugs. Thus do addictions begin. (Yes, art can be an addiction.) So what does one do with this moment of timelessness when one is back in time?

Friedrich Nietzsche felt that this distinction between time and timelessness was itself a primary metaphysical problem, and weakness. To isolate any one moment outside of time, to privilege it above all others, even to *want* such a thing—all this is to betray, and be defeated by, time itself. Joy, though inevitably tragic because death is absolute, is the very lifeblood of being and ought to be sought and seized at *every* moment of existence. It is an extreme philosophy which few could follow, though there is one poet in this book, the good old rock-eating, human-hating Robinson Jeffers, who actually saw Nietzsche's scathing wager, and raised it:

> Though joy is better than sorrow joy is not great;
> Peace is great, strength is great.

Not for joy the stars burn, not for joy the vulture
Spreads her gray sails on the air
Over the mountain; not for joy the worn mountain
Stands, while years like water
Trench his long sides. "I am neither mountain nor bird
Nor star; and I seek joy."
The weakness of your breed: yet at length quietness
Will cover those wistful eyes.

For Jeffers the whole notion of joy is misguided and suggests some moral rot at the center of the species. Better to live like the stars and the mountain, the dark vulture hovering watchfully over the weaker meats.

These criticisms are at once bracing and frustrating. It's worth having one's spiritual complacency—whether it's a too-modest sense of one's own existential power and volition or a too-easy sinking into an oceanic oneness with the universe—checked. It's worth being reminded—and made to *feel*—besides its splendor, the brute, material necessity that is also at the heart of being, as well as the agency we retain when being crushed by it. But are we to assume, then, as Jeffers insists, that our moments of heightened awareness and communion are illusions, or that, *pace* Nietzsche, they merely show what we ought to be feeling at every second? What would it really look like to live with such molecular indifference or constant existential orgasm?

I suspect that for most of us the "ache" at the end of Wilbur's poem, the longing that "nothing can satisfy," will seem all too familiar and, no matter how much or how little "faith" we have, ineradicable. Wilbur himself, after all, is a practicing Christian. He may very well mean "nothing but God," but the poem is careful not to say that, and its reticence is not merely a matter of form and modern metaphysical decorum. To state such a thing, to name the experience and its source in such an authoritative way, would be to betray everything that made the experience what it was. The question that Wilbur's poem raises, then, the question that many of the poems in this book raise, remains: *now what?*

6.

> *We wander*
> *the roof of hell*
> *choosing blossoms.*

KOBAYASHI ISSA
(TRANSLATED BY
JANE HIRSHFIELD)

And this is where that earlier objection becomes germane: namely, that even to speak of joy in these times, much less to claim to feel it—and much, much less to exhort *others* to feel it—might be an obscenity in the face of so much human suffering. Jack Gilbert's poem "A Brief for the Defense" addresses this issue directly.

> Sorrow everywhere. Slaughter everywhere. If babies
> are not starving someplace, they are starving
> somewhere else. With flies in their nostrils.
> But we enjoy our lives because that's what God wants.

The irony is a rhetorical strategy here (the title tells us we're in a trial, after all), designed to elicit liberal sympathies with a shared smirk. Those idiot Christians, one thinks, taking all those New Testament injunctions to rejoice as excuses to consume, yee-hawing out of a million megachurches like elated locusts. The speaker of Gilbert's poem knows full well the strangeness, the apparent offensiveness, of his message (as would have, by the way, those early audiences of Paul and others, many of whom might very well have made their way home past rows of crucified corpses designed specifically to eradicate all cause for any insurrectionist hope or joy). There is joy in the gutters of Calcutta, Gilbert's speaker says, and the sex slaves laugh in the cages of Bombay. I suppose these things are true, but they are so remote and exotic that they are likely to seem, for the typical reader of this poem, like props. Again, this is for effect, mirroring the way we tend to reach for extreme examples—like Ivan with his newspaper clippings of atrocities in *The Brothers Karamazov*—when arguing about ethics or theodicy. When the heart of the argument comes, it does so with such knowing clarity—and, for modern poetry, such rare, sincere didacticism—that it feels like we are no longer judge or jury, but in the dock:

> If we deny our happiness, resist our satisfaction,
> we lessen the importance of their deprivation.
> We must risk delight. We can do without pleasure,
> but not delight. Not enjoyment. We must have
> the stubbornness to accept our gladness in the ruthless
> furnace of this world. To make injustice the only
> measure of our attention is to praise the Devil.
> If the locomotive of the Lord runs us down,
> we should give thanks that the end had magnitude.

Back to irony, just a tad, in those last two lines, but the more intimate and immediate argument, the one that bears on our daily lives, has been delivered. Joy is the only inoculation against the despair to which any sane person is prone, the only antidote to the nihilism that wafts through our intellectual atmosphere like sarin gas. More than that: Joy is what keeps reality from being sufficient unto itself, which is to say, it is what keeps reality *real,* since in this world of multiverses and quantum weirdness, where ninety-five percent of matter and energy we know only to name as "dark," it is obvious that reality extends far beyond what our senses can perceive. So what in the world, or what beyond the world, is calling to us when we are called to joy? "It is true that the unknown is the largest need of the intellect," wrote Emily Dickinson in a letter, "though for it, no one ever thinks to thank God."

7.

For poets—and maybe for all artists after Romanticism—Gilbert's poem can't help but bring to mind an artistic and psychological dynamic that has become so much a part of collective conscious-ness that artists themselves can become unconscious of the extent to which their work is burdened by it. *Light writes white,* as the old saying goes. I have seen this expression attributed to numerous writers, including (and this may be the most likely source) the anon-ymous ones of Tin Pan Alley. In any event, you get the idea: if all is well with your life, if you have around you every creature comfort, including some dear creature you love more than art, then when you sit down to make said art what you will find is . . . white: the page stays blank. Art emerges out of tension, the thinking goes, out of absence and lack. It is always the expression of, and always the only remedy to, some essential insufficiency. For the true artist, then, to slip into happiness is to betray one's nature. "What is a poet?" asked

Kierkegaard. "An unhappy person who conceals profound anguish in his heart but whose lips are so formed that as sighs and cries pass over them they sound like beautiful music."

No doubt there's some truth to this idea, which is itself beautifully formulated (and for Kierkegaard, one suspects, that most literary of philosophers, a bit wistfully reflexive and self-exonerating). If language separates us from the world it makes available, if even joy brings its own unique grief, it follows that to be conscious at all is to be conscious of loss. But this is what a man in my childhood used to call a watermelon wisdom: sweet in pieces but hell to swallow whole.

The one abundance you can count on in this life is lack. An artist need not go looking for it, much less empowering it unnaturally by laying her gift down in front of sadness like a sacrifice. If anything, a modern artist might have to lean the other way, might have to seek out and sing her moments of happiness and joy, if only to balance the scale. Robert Lowell, who suffered from manic-depression and became as famous for his miseries as for his verse—indeed the two can be very difficult to disentangle—said late in his life that, when looking back, what he chiefly remembered was the happiness. This is not entirely surprising if you read Lowell's biography, for he was a caring and charismatic person, capable of genuine relationships of all kinds. No, the surprise comes when reading through the thousand or so pages of Lowell's collected poems, which reveal no hint of that happiness—quite the opposite, actually. "We asked to be obsessed with writing/and we were," Lowell wrote, a bit ruefully, in a late elegy to John Berryman. But surely if what one most remembers and values from a life is the happiness, and one's lifelong obsession has entirely failed to capture that, then in some major way it has failed. Here's how that Gilbert poem ends:

> To hear the faint sound of oars in the silence as a rowboat
> comes slowly out and then goes back is truly worth
> all the years of sorrow that are to come.

8.

But there is a limitation to that Gilbert poem too. Lovely as that last image is, and as true as it is in terms of establishing relative values in one's own emotional and aesthetic economy, it still sits somewhat uneasily against the early images of suffering. It may very well be the case that one moment of true communion with reality, one moment of joy, is worth all the suffering that one must undergo, but is it also true that one's enjoyment is worth the suffering of others, however extreme? Of course it isn't, and the poem is aimed directly at the fallacy of this calculus. I do feel, though, that the poem avoids, or fails to account for, the revolutionary force of pure joy. Or rather the revolutionary force of a joy that, in this world, is inevitably impure, compounded as it is of eternity and time, praise and pain. As the theologian Jürgen Moltmann writes:

> Joy in life's happiness motivates us to revolt against the life that is de-
> stroyed and against those who destroy life. And grief over life that is
> destroyed is nothing other than an ardent longing for life's liberation
> to happiness and joy. Otherwise we would accept innocent suffering
> and destroyed life as our fate and destiny. Compassion is the other
> side of the living joy. We don't accuse God because there is suffering

in the world. Rather, we protest in the name of God against suffering and those who cause it.

Compassion is the other side of the living joy. Yes, and compassion can include fury and lead to action. This is why Sterling Brown's poem "Slim in Atlanta" belongs in this anthology. Brown imagines a world in which "niggers" (to avoid the word would be to betray the poem) must do all of their laughing—must express all of their joy—closed up in telephone booths. Slim finds this so outlandishly hilarious that he has to bolt to the front of the line and close himself up inside the booth so he can explode. He laughs so hard and for so long that eventually he has to be taken away by ambulance. The poem ends:

De state paid de railroad
    To take him away;
Den, things was as usural
    In Atlanta, Gee A.

"Slim in Atlanta" was written in the 1930s, when Jim Crow laws extended into every aspect of Southern society and were enforced with a contagious brutality. Never mind the separate lunch counters and drinking fountains; simply failing to yield the right of way to a white driver could result in a beating. Or worse. Lynchings were still common and sometimes involved not simply the "perpetrator" but family and friends as well. In 1946, not far from Atlanta, a white mob, upset that a black man accused of attacking a white man had been granted bail, killed the suspect, his wife, and another African-American couple on hand. Still unsated, and rightly certain of their immunity (not a single charge was ever filed), they cut the fetus out of the woman, who had been pregnant, and made sure it was dead too. Not so funny anymore, old Slim, whose acid laughter and weaponized irony (the "fake" dialect is part of this) are a long way from Gilbert's lonely, consoling rowboat under the stars. "If we warn against irony as a seducer," says Kierkegaard, "we must also praise it as a guide."

9.

> *Azure lobelia props up the heart*
> *that extra hair's breadth happiness is.*

PETER COLE

Happiness? Or is Cole in fact describing a moment of joy? The literature distinguishing between the two is extensive, and writers from Aristotle to C. S. Lewis have tended to draw a stark line. Happiness is a disposition or evaluation: we are happy when we experience pleasure, when things go our way, and so on. Joy, by contrast, is an emotion: there is always an element of having been *seized*. Happiness involves enlarging or securing the self: you're happy when you pay off your mortgage or get a raise. Joy, by contrast, always involves some loss of self, from the parent reveling in the autonomous existence of her child to the contemplative lost in religious ecstasy (which some philosophers actually distinguish from joy).

I have waited until now to make this sharp distinction for the same reason I have confined it to a single paragraph: I'm not sure the distinction is quite so sharp. Sometimes joy really can be an intensification of happiness. It can crown and ratify a flourishing life (as in Grace Paley's "Here"), or be the spiritual fruition of a happiness that is not quite grasped or realized (Sarah Lindsay) or is gone

(Gwendolyn Brooks's "the rites for Cousin Vit"). But joy can also compromise, even obliterate, happiness. It can reveal a happiness to be so hopelessly tenuous and shallow that, on the other side of the rupture, you can find yourself with no tenable—or at least no honorable—way back. Or it can disclose a spiritual existence the full realization of which will require some sacrifice—of a very real happiness, say. But to acknowledge that the line is sometimes there is not to admit that it always is. In any event, poetry does not usually refine philosophical definitions so much as weaken one's need to see them, even as it strengthens the intuitive trust, tolerance for paradox, and general spiritual fluency that are required to thrive without such definitions.

Some poems, though—and thus some experiences—do demand one term or the other. When Maria Hummel, in her poem "Station," describes a moment of tender but terrifying intimacy with her chronically sick son, the keenest shock may be not for the calm control she exercises formally and emotionally, but for the presence in this sobering poem of that one word "joy." "Days you are sick, we get dressed slow," Hummel writes, before they head to the hospital:

> Burlingame is the size of joy:
> a race past bakeries, gold rings
> in open black cases. I don't care
> who sees my crooked smile
>
> or what erases it, past the bakery,
> when you tire. We ride the blades again
> beside the crooked bay. You smile.
> I hold you like a hole holds light.

We wear our hats and ride the knives.
They cannot fix you. They try and try.
Tunnel! Into the dark open we go.
Days you are sick, we get dressed slow.

Few things are more wrenching—or more hopeful—than a child's innocent delight in the midst of devastation. There is no happiness in "Station," but in the strong charge between mother and son, in the provisional haven their love makes of danger ("We wear our hats and ride the knives"), there is a joy that is entirely credible and genuinely consoling. And maybe even redemptive? Who cries out that word *Tunnel*? The mother? The boy? It almost seems an utterance of Love itself, which opens the darkness into which they are headed, or makes them, faced with such terrible darkness, open to whatever saving grace might be there, and only there. *Into the dark open we go.*

By contrast, consider this little poem by the Italian modernist Trilussa, beautifully translated by John DuVal:

A bee settled
on a rose petal.
It sipped, and off it flew.
All in all, happiness, too,
is something little.

This seems a very similar experience to the one depicted by Cole—there is even another flower to prop the heart. Neither poet is defining happiness so much as testing that abstraction against reality. But Cole's poem enables one (or enables me, at any rate) to forget the distinction between joy and happiness, to let each mean, for a moment, the other. Trilussa's use of the word is both more precise and less . . . expansive, perhaps, which is to say less troubling, since under the hair's breadth of happiness in Cole's poem there is, one can't help but feel, an unhappiness, or maybe just a lack of happiness, that is much more common. Perhaps it comes down to this: you would not say of joy that it is "something little," even when the details that give rise to it seem almost too ordinary to notice, as with Cole's poem, or as with this eerie, holy anti-elegy by Donald Hall:

> In June's high light she stood at the sink
> 　　With a glass of wine,
> And listened for the bobolink,
> And crushed garlic in late sunshine.
>
> I watched her cooking, from my chair.
> 　　She pressed her lips
> Together, reached for kitchenware,
> And tasted sauce from her fingertips.
>
> "It's ready now. Come on," she said.
> 　　"You light the candle."
> We ate, and talked, and went to bed,
> And slept. It was a miracle.

Where is the joy here? In the past, when all of the daily details went mostly unnoticed, as they inevitably do for all of us—and when they constituted, one assumes, a sustained happiness? (The poem purports to memorialize a particular day, but it's significant that there is no particular thing to mark this day out as being different from others.) Or is the joy in the present, when the day has been re-created by language—note how ordinary the words and rhythms are, how workaday, how like a life well used—and the full fact of what one has been given, and what one has lost, is suddenly apparent: "It was a miracle." The poem strives to say, strives to be true to, the combination of love and lament, grace and loss, that arises in us when we feel to the very last atom of our existence an existence that is now elsewhere.

10.

> *The happiness of refusing happiness*
> *The joy of refusing joy*
> *Passionately keeping passion back*
> *Proudly breaking pride in ecstasy*

AVROM LYESIN

(TRANSLATED BY

ZACKARY SHOLEM BERGER)

For all of the poets I've discussed so far, and for most of the poets in this book, a moment of joy is, or at least leads to, a moment of comprehension. We "see into the life of things." Being becomes "a thing to understand." Implicit within them is an assumption that existence is something that can *be* understood, even if only in spots of time. "It was the last nostalgia," wrote that great musical metaphysician Wallace Stevens, "that he/should understand."

There is another step some poets have taken (including, at times, Stevens), the joy not of discovering meaning but of being released from it, freed from the need to make meaning, freed even from the word and concept of meaning. This is the atmosphere of the "precisely pointless" discipline of Craig Arnold's poem "Meditation on a Grapefruit," which was written not long before Arnold, one of the most vital and charismatic people I have ever known, vanished forever while exploring a volcano in Japan. It is the Zen calm of Jane Hirshfield's "Once, I," with its "lovers so happy/neither needs think of the other." These poets are not "seeing into the life of things" so much as simply seeing. There is no "meaning" to extract from these poems without deforming them, yet the ghost of that word ripples off the simple descriptions like heat.

And then there is another step: the joy of the void, the rash dance of despair itself, the seizing of even utmost loneliness as occasion to roar, rage, maybe even praise. Praise what? Survival, says Stanley Kunitz, who died in 2006 at the raw wild age of one hundred. Or being the living soul of one's own lonely domain, as a naked, capering William Carlos Williams proclaims in "Danse Russe":

if I in my north room
dance naked, grotesquely
before my mirror
waving my shirt round my head
and singing softly to myself:
"I am lonely, lonely.
I was born to be lonely,
I am best so!"
If I admire my arms, my face,
my shoulders, flanks, buttocks
against the yellow drawn shades,—

Who shall say I am not
the happy genius of my household?

This strain of song is not necessarily modern. It's this antic and just-this-side-of-sanity current that crackles through *Lear.* Nor is it nihilism, as the sheer force of imagination in such work bespeaks, at its heart, creation and not destruction, life and not death. Or, perhaps more accurately, such work speaks those apparent opposites into a feeling so fused that the distinctions fall away, or fall into what one might call, always a little helplessly, God, as in the conclusion to this nineteenth-century sonnet by Frederick Goddard Tuckerman:

No more thy meaning seek, thine anguish plead,
But leaving straining thought and stammering word
Across the barren azure pass to God,
Shooting the void in silence like a bird—
A bird that shuts its wings for better speed.

One cannot choose to suffer—and it does involve suffering—this last step. That results in degradation, not transformation. But there are indeed some poets, like some people, who must learn to spend everything on nothing. And there are some poems, like some lives, in which nothing, like the very Void out of which matter first emerged, *happens*.

11.

> The might
> to move what her eye fell upon
> is the image of her I keep,
> her iridescent readiness.

W. S. DI PIERO

I hope it's apparent by this point that poetry itself—the making of it, certainly, but also the remaking of it as the reader—is often a form of joy. Indeed, in C. S. Lewis's famous memoir *Surprised by Joy,* an early encounter with poetry is one of the three experiences of disabling/enabling joy to which he attributes his eventual conversion. Lewis describes a seismic shock, the kind that happens only a handful of times in one's life. Certainly there are lesser joys, which are still clearly distinguishable from mere pleasure. After years of living with "Tintern Abbey," I still feel a transcendent shiver from the poem, partly because it describes so well experiences that I have had in my life, but mostly because of the soul-conjuring and soul-compelling currents of the verse itself, the terrestrial fidelity married to atmospheric immensity, the way one feels, as Wordsworth puts it in *The Prelude,* the "huge and mighty forms" of nature that "move slowly through the mind," and are the mind.

"That joy could be reborn out of the annihilation of the individual is only comprehensible from the spirit of music." Thus Nietzsche again. And thus Gerard Manley Hopkins, who updates Wordsworth by making some aspect of nature, and thus of God, in some way dormant, quiescent, even expectant, until it is catalyzed by human consciousness:

> These things, these things were here and but the beholder
> Wanting; which two when they once meet,
> The heart rears wings bold and bolder
> And hurls for him, O half hurls earth for him off under his feet.

Thus Kay Ryan, who peers stoically, jokingly—but hopefully!—into the abyss of oblivion to find her "ideal audience," who is just one person, perhaps, maybe not even born yet, maybe long dead, but who in any event

> will know with
> exquisite gloom
> that only we two
> ever found this room.

Thus Fanny Howe's "ecstatic lash/of the poetic line," and whatever it is that "freaks/forth a bluet" for James Schuyler, and the "Sweet sweet

sweet sweet sweet tea" (it's that last "sweet" that's inspired) that Gertrude Stein uses to describe a Spanish Flamenco dancer in 1913:

> Sweet sweet sweet sweet sweet tea.
>   Susie Asado.
> Susie Asado which is a told tray sure.
> A lean on the shoe this means slips slips hers.
> When the ancient light grey is clean it is yellow, it is a silver seller.

Obviously, one is not meant to understand this in the way one understands a newspaper article or even in the way one understands most poetry. You are meant to get lost in its vertiginous precisions, the weird syncopations of syntax and skin. You are meant to feel something of what Stein felt: joy.

That tired word. Appropriated by Fifth Avenue and the Third Reich (the Nazis had a real affinity for, and belief in, the raw power of *Freude*), used to peddle soap and salvation, the word requires some work to rehabilitate. (As do, no doubt, the many discriminations of emotion that the word encompasses.) When I was reading for this anthology, it was perhaps most gratifying to come across poems where I didn't expect to find them: the hard-won somber celebration of life by that uber-Grinch Philip Larkin in "Coming," the weird ride on God taken by the sacred atheist (and Holocaust survivor) Paul Celan in "With wine and being lost, with," the unabashed admiration and adoration that Sylvia Plath—already neck-deep in the rising waters of sorrow that would soon take her in—lavishes on her child in "You're."

> Snug as a bud and at home
> Like a sprat in a pickle jug.
> A creel of eels, all ripples.

Jumpy as a Mexican bean.
Right, like a well-done sum.
A clean slate, with your own face on.

Joy: that durable, inexhaustible, essential, inadequate word.
That something in the soul that makes one able to claim again the
word "soul." That sensation more exalting than happiness, less
graspable than hope, though both of these feelings are implicated,
challenged, changed. That seed of being which can bud even in our
"circumstance of ice," as Danielle Chapman puts it, so that faith
suddenly is not something one need contemplate, struggle for, or
even "have," really, but is simply there, as the world is there. There
is no way to plan for, much less conjure, such an experience. One
can only, like Lucille Clifton—who in the decade during which I was
responsible for awarding the annual Ruth Lilly Prize in Poetry for
lifetime achievement was the one person who let out a spontaneous
yawp of delight on the phone—try to make oneself fit to feel the
moment when it comes, and let it carry you where it will:

why
is what i ask myself
maybe it is the afrikan in me
still trying to get home
after all these years
but when i wake to the heat of morning
galloping down the highway of my life
something hopeful rises in me
rises and runs me out into the road
and i lob my fierce thigh high
over the rump of the day and honey
i ride   i ride

A NOTE ON THE SELECTIONS

I have limited my selections for this anthology to poets born during or after modernism. I wanted a diversity of voices, first of all. Our individual histories and ethnicities may not entirely determine our experiences and expressions of joy, but surely they matter. Representing that diversity—in English-language poetry, at least—has become possible only in the past hundred years or so.

Also, I wanted specifically to explore what joy means for poets at this moment in history. My sense is that many writers have come to distrust the word—no doubt because they have come to distrust, or at least be confused by, the feeling. I also sense, though—and I hope this anthology bears it out—that some unconscious effort at recovery is taking place. And since poets are after all, as Ezra Pound assured us, "the antennae of the race," maybe this recovery is more general.

I have made exceptions in my selections for Emily Dickinson and Gerard Manley Hopkins. Both these writers acutely and uniquely anticipated modernism, and both had to wait for modernism to find their audience. It would seem strange not to have their voices present.

In addition to the one hundred poems, I have included a number of quotations from other texts. Most of these are from the prose of poets, but some are from works of theology, philosophy, natural science, and correspondence. These are intended to inflect individual poems or groups of poems in different ways. Some of the quotations contradict each other and/or points I have made in my introduction, which seems inevitable and necessary for any book that is not meant to be an argument, but an experience.

JOY

FIRST SONG

Then it was dusk in Illinois, the small boy
After an afternoon of carting dung
Hung on the rail fence, a sapped thing
Weary to crying. Dark was growing tall
And he began to hear the pond frogs all
Calling on his ear with what seemed their joy.

Soon their sound was pleasant for a boy
Listening in the smoky dusk and the nightfall
Of Illinois, and from the fields two small
Boys came bearing cornstalk violins
And they rubbed the cornstalk bows with resins
And the three sat there scraping of their joy.

It was now fine music the frogs and the boys
Did in the towering Illinois twilight make
And into dark in spite of a shoulder's ache
A boy's hunched body loved out of a stalk
The first song of his happiness, and the song woke
His heart to the darkness and into the sadness of joy.

GALWAY KINNELL

3

from THE PRECISION OF PAIN AND THE BLURRINESS OF JOY: THE TOUCH OF LONGING IS EVERYWHERE

20

The precision of pain and the blurriness of joy. I'm thinking
how precise people are when they describe their pain in a doctor's
   office.
Even those who haven't learned to read and write are precise:
"This one's a throbbing pain, that one's a wrenching pain,
this one gnaws, that one burns, this is a sharp pain
and that—a dull one. Right here. Precisely here,
yes, yes." Joy blurs everything. I've heard people say
after nights of love and feasting, "It was great,
I was in seventh heaven." Even the spaceman who floated
in outer space, tethered to a spaceship, could say only, "Great,
wonderful, I have no words."
The blurriness of joy and the precision of pain—
I want to describe, with a sharp pain's precision, happiness
and blurry joy. I learned to speak among the pains.

YEHUDA AMICHAI

(TRANSLATED FROM THE HEBREW BY

CHANA BLOCH AND CHANA KRONFELD)

CANAL BANK WALK

Leafy-with-love banks and the green waters of the canal
Pouring redemption for me, that I do
The will of God, wallow in the habitual, the banal,
Grow with nature again as before I grew.
The bright stick trapped, the breeze adding a third
Party to the couple kissing on an old seat,
And a bird gathering materials for the nest for the Word
Eloquently new and abandoned to its delirious beat.
O unworn world enrapture me, encapture me in a web
Of fabulous grass and eternal voices by a beech,
Feed the gaping need of my senses, give me ad lib
To pray unselfconsciously with overflowing speech
For this soul needs to be honoured with a new dress woven
From green and blue things and arguments that cannot be proven.

PATRICK KAVANAGH

The reality of any joy in the world is indescribable, only in joy does creation happen (happiness, on the contrary, is only a promising and interpretable pattern of things already existing); joy, however, is a marvelous increasing of what already exists, a pure addition out of nothingness. How superficially must happiness engage us, after all, if it can leave us time to think and worry about how long it will last. Joy is a moment, unobligated, timeless from the beginning, not to be held but also not to be truly lost again, since under its impact our being is changed chemically, so to speak, and does not only, as may be the case with happiness, savor and enjoy itself in a new mixture.

RAINER MARIA RILKE,
LETTER TO ILSE ERDMANN,
JANUARY 31, 1914

THIS IS US SAINT'S DAY

This is us Saint's Day. This is us Saint's Day.
The frescoed snow makes it that way,
the yellow haloes scraped by the tethers—

Benedice.

Bring palms.
Hands to hotly breathing bless.
Pass by Cut Paws and Kennel Cough—
prayer's the run, hell's the kennel—
they coughcough steam,
their agony dwindle.

The sled jerk and the skids crease down hard
and every dog is baying for a six minute run—
broiling bellies in snow, snapping jaws on snow,
drilling pissholes in snow—Deo! Deo!

Hup! Hup! Hup!

Yodelling Gloria as we run, sled-dogs jamp
like strangled surf towards heaven.

JEN HADFIELD

TRAVELIN' SHOES

And at last, I get the phone call. The blues rolls into
my sleepy ears at five A.M., a dry, official voice from
my father's hospital. A question, a few quick facts,
and my daddy's lying upstate on the coolin' floor.

Death, it seems, was kinder to him in his last hour
than life was in his last four months.

Death, who pulls him to a low ebb, then slowly
floods over his wrecked body like a lover.

Cardio-vascular collapse, the polite voice is telling
me, but later my cousin tells me, he arrives on the
ward before they shut my father's eyes and mouth to
see the joy still resting on his face from the moment
my daddy finally split his misery open.

CORNELIUS EADY

THE BLESSING OF THE OLD WOMAN,
THE TULIP, AND THE DOG

To be blessed
said the old woman
is to live and work
so hard
God's love
washes right through you
like milk through a cow

To be blessed
said the dark red tulip
is to knock their eyes out
with the slug of lust
implied by
your up-ended
skirt

To be blessed
said the dog
is to have a pinch
of God
inside you
and all the other
dogs can smell it

ALICIA SUSKIN OSTRIKER

How can I number the worlds to which the eye gives me entry?—the world of light, of colour, of shape, of shadow: of mathematical precision in the snowflake, the ice formation, the quartz crystal, the patterns of stamen and petal: of rhythm in the fluid curve and plunging line of the mountain faces. Why some blocks of stone, hacked into violent and tortured shapes, should so profoundly tranquilise the mind I do not know. Perhaps the eye imposes its own rhythm on what is only a confusion: one has to look creatively to see this mass of rock as more than jag and pinnacle—as beauty. Else why did men for so many centuries think mountains repulsive? A certain kind of consciousness interacts with the mountain-forms to create this sense of beauty. Yet the forms must be there for the eye to see. And forms of a certain distinction: mere dollops won't do it. It is, as with all creation, matter impregnated with mind: but the resultant issue is a living spirit, a glow in the consciousness, that perishes when the glow is dead. It is something snatched from non-being, that shadow which creeps in on us continuously and can be held off by continuous creative act. So, simply to look on anything, such as a mountain, with the love that penetrates to its essence, is to widen the domain of being in the vastness of non-being. Man has no other reason for his existence.

NAN SHEPHERD, *The Living Mountain*

HAMLEN BROOK

At the alder-darkened brink
Where the stream slows to a lucid jet
I lean to the water, dinting its top with sweat,
And see, before I can drink,

A startled inchling trout
Of spotted near-transparency,
Trawling a shadow solider than he.
He swerves now, darting out

To where, in a flicked slew
Of sparks and glittering silt, he weaves
Through stream-bed rocks, disturbing foundered leaves,
And butts then out of view

Beneath a sliding glass
Crazed by the skimming of a brace
Of burnished dragon-flies across its face,
In which deep cloudlets pass

And a white precipice
Of mirrored birch-trees plunges down
Toward where the azures of the zenith drown.
How shall I drink all this?

Joy's trick is to supply
Dry lips with what can cool and slake,
Leaving them dumbstruck also with an ache
Nothing can satisfy.

RICHARD WILBUR

HAG RIDING

why
is what i ask myself
maybe it is the afrikan in me
still trying to get home
after all these years
but when i wake to the heat of morning
galloping down the highway of my life
something hopeful rises in me
rises and runs me out into the road
and i lob my fierce thigh high
over the rump of the day and honey
i ride   i ride

LUCILLE CLIFTON

SMALL MOTH

She's slicing ripe white peaches
into the Tony the Tiger bowl
and dropping slivers for the dog
poised vibrating by her foot to stop their fall
when she spots it, camouflaged,
a glimmer and then full on—
happiness, plashing blunt soft wings
inside her as if it wants
to escape again.

SARAH LINDSAY

AND WE LOVE LIFE

And we love life if we find a way to it.
We dance in between martyrs and raise a minaret for violet or palm
  trees.

We love life if we find a way to it.

And we steal from the silkworm a thread to build a sky and fence in
  this departure.
We open the garden gate for the jasmine to go out as a beautiful day
  on the streets.

We love life if we find a way to it.

And we plant, where we settle, some fast growing plants, and har-
  vest the dead.
We play the flute like the color of the faraway, sketch over the dirt
  corridor a neigh.
We write our names one stone at a time, O lightning make the night
  a bit clearer.

We love life if we find a way to it . . .

MAHMOUD DARWISH
(TRANSLATED FROM THE
ARABIC BY FADY JOUDAH)

TO MAKE A SUMMER

Barney says his high-school daughter
Keeps exclaiming joy, joy.
The burden of my joy lightens
With her exclamation.

It's a generality, it takes
From my heart the sting of the singular, it sets moving
In the easy early Berkeley air
What we incommunicably share.

JOSEPHINE MILES

THE CROWD

It is not given to everyone to blend into the multitude: enjoying the crowd is an art, and only he can gain a stroke of vitality from it, at humanity's expense, whose good fairy at his cradle bequeathed a taste for travesty and masque, along with hatred of home and passion for travel.

Multitude, solitude: equal and convertible terms for the active and productive poet. Those who cannot people their solitude can never be alone in a busy crowd.

The poet rejoices in this incomparable privilege, that he can, at will, be both himself and another. Like a lost soul searching for a body, he enters when he wishes into any character. For him all is vacancy; and if certain places appear to shut him out, in his eye they are not worth a visit.

Who walks alone with his thoughts draws a singular intoxication from this universal communion. Whoever readily commingles with the crowd knows feverish pleasures eternally denied to the egoist, locked like a strongbox, or the sloth, confined like the snail. He takes on himself all professions, all the joys and all the miseries that circumstances hand him.

What men call love is petty, limited, feeble compared with this ineffable orgy, with this sacred whoredom of the soul which renders itself entire, poetry and charity, to the sudden unexpected, to the passing unknown.

It is good sometimes to remind the favored of this world, were it only to bring down their stupid pride, that there are felicities greater than theirs, larger, more refined. Founders of colonies, pastors of their people, missionaries exiled to the end of the world, no doubt know something of these mysterious intoxications; and in the bosom of the vast family that their spirit has formed, they must sometimes laugh at those who pity their so troubled fortunes and so chaste lives.

CHARLES BAUDELAIRE

(TRANSLATED FROM THE FRENCH BY KEITH WALDROP)

THE DANCING

In all these rotten shops, in all this broken furniture
and wrinkled ties and baseball trophies and coffee pots
I have never seen a postwar Philco
with the automatic eye
nor heard Ravel's "Bolero" the way I did
in 1945 in that tiny living room
on Beechwood Boulevard, nor danced as I did
then, my knives all flashing, my hair all streaming,
my mother red with laughter, my father cupping
his left hand under his armpit, doing the dance
of old Ukraine, the sound of his skin half drum,
half fart, the world at last a meadow,
the three of us whirling and singing, the three of us
screaming and falling, as if we were dying,
as if we could never stop—in 1945—
in Pittsburgh, beautiful filthy Pittsburgh, home
of the evil Mellons, 5,000 miles away
from the other dancing—in Poland and Germany—
oh God of mercy, oh wild God.

GERALD STERN

WITH WINE AND BEING LOST, WITH

With wine and being lost, with
less and less of both:

I rode through the snow, do you read me,
I rode God far—I rode God
near, he sang,
it was
our last ride over
the hurdled humans.

They cowered when
they heard us
overhead, they
wrote, they
lied our neighing
into one of their
image-ridden languages.

PAUL CELAN

(TRANSLATED FROM THE GERMAN BY
NIKOLAI POPOV AND HEATHER MCHUGH)

There must be someone to live through it all and bear witness to the fact that God lived, even in these times.

ETTY HILLESUM, Diaries

What can we say about God? Nothing. What can we say *to* God? Everything. Poems to God are prayer. And if there are no prayers nowadays . . . it is not because we don't have anything to say to God, nor because we have no one to say this anything to—there is something and there is someone—but because we haven't the conscience to praise and pray God in the same language we've used for centuries to praise and pray absolutely everything. In our age, to have the courage for direct speech to God (for prayer) we must either not know what poems are, or forget.

MARINA TSVETAEVA, Art in the Light of Conscience

OUT AT LANESVILLE

In memoriam Mary Ann, 1932–1980

The five or six of them, sitting on the rocks
Out at Lanesville, near Gloucester; it is like
Listening to music. Several of them are teachers,
One is a psychologist, one is reading a book,
The page glares white in the summer sunlight;
Others are just sunning themselves, or just
Sitting there looking out over the water;
A couple of them seem to be talking together;
From this far off you can't hear what they are saying.

The day is hot, the absolute middle of summer.
Someone has written an obscenity
In huge letters on the rocks above and behind
This group of people, and someone else, one of them,
Maybe, or maybe a neighbor, the owner of one
Of the cottages up behind and back in the woods,
Has tried to erase it and only partly done so,
So that for years it will say hoarsely FUCK
To the random winds and to the senseless waves.

One of them is sitting with her back turned
To me and to the others on the rocks. The purple
Loosestrife and the tigerlilies are like the flags
Of some celebration; they bloom along the edge
Of a small stream that makes its way unseen
Down to the rocks and sand. Her shoulders are round,
And rather luxuriously heavy, and the whole figure

Has a youthful and graceful amplitude of being
Whose beauty will last her her whole life long.

The voices of some people out in a boat somewhere
Are carried in over the water with surprising
Force and clarity, though saying I don't know what:
Happiness; unhappiness; something about the conditions
Of all such things; work done, not done; the saving
Of the self in the intense work of its singleness,
Learning to live with it. Their lives have separate ends.
Suddenly she turns her head and seems to look
Toward me and toward the others on the rocks,

So that her body, turned away, is more expressive
Than her blank face, a pure reflector of light.

DAVID FERRY

The knowledge of the fallen world does not kill joy, which emanates in this world, always, constantly, as a bright sorrow.

ALEXANDER SCHMEMANN

The Journals of Father Alexander Schmemann

THE BLUET

And is it stamina
that unseasonably freaks
forth a bluet, a
Quaker lady, by
the lake? So small,
a drop of sky that
splashed and held,
four-petaled, creamy
in its throat. The woods
around were brown,
the air crisp as a
Carr's table water
biscuit and smelt of
cider. There were frost
apples on the trees in
the field below the house.
The pond was still, then
broke into a ripple.
The hills, the leaves that
have not yet fallen
are deep and oriental
rug colors. Brown leaves
in the woods set off
gray trunks of trees.
But that bluet was
the focus of it all: last
spring, next spring, what
does it matter? Unexpected
as a tear when someone

reads a poem you wrote
for him: "It's this line
here." That bluet breaks
me up, tiny spring flower
late, late in dour October.

JAMES SCHUYLER

HIP-HOP GHAZAL

Gotta love us brown girls, munching on fat, swinging blue hips,
decked out in shells and splashes, Lawdie, bringing them woo hips.

As the jukebox teases, watch my sistas throat the heartbreak,
inhaling bassline, cracking backbone and singing thru hips.

Like something boneless, we glide silent, seeping 'tween floorboards,
wrapping around the hims, and *ooh wee,* clinging like glue hips.

Engines grinding, rotating, smokin', gotta pull back some.
Natural minds are lost at the mere sight of ringing true hips.

Gotta love us girls, just struttin' down Manhattan streets
killing the menfolk with a dose of that stinging view. Hips.

Crying 'bout getting old—Patricia, you need to get up off
what God gave you. Say a prayer and start slinging. Cue hips.

PATRICIA SMITH

TEMPTATION

Call yourself alive? Look, I promise you
that for the first time you'll feel your pores opening
like fish mouths, and you'll actually be able to hear
your blood surging through all those lanes,
and you'll feel light gliding across the cornea
like the train of a dress. For the first time
you'll be aware of gravity
like a thorn in your heel,
and your shoulder blades will ache for want of wings.
Call yourself alive? I promise you
you'll be deafened by the sound of dust falling on furniture,
you'll feel your eyebrows turning to two gashes,
and every memory you have—will begin
at Genesis.

NINA CASSIAN

(TRANSLATED FROM THE ROMANIAN

BY BRENDA WALKER AND ANDREA DELETANT)

LOONY-BIN BASKETBALL

The gym opened out
before us like a vast arena, the bleached floorboards
yawned toward a vanishing point, staggered seats high
as the Mayan temple I once saw devoured by vines.
Each of us was eaten up inside—all citizens of lost
       and unmapped cities.

Frank hugged the pimply ball
over his belly like an unborn child. Claire
dressed for daycare in daffodil yellow and jelly shoes.
David's gaze was an emperor's surveying a desiccated
battlefield. Since he viewed everything that way, we all
       saw him the same.

The psych techs in Cloroxed white
were giant angels who set us running drills, at which
we sucked. The zones we set out to defend were watery
at every edge. We missed close chest passes, easy combos.
Our metronomes run different tempos,
       John proclaimed.

Then Claire started seeing
dashes stutter through the air behind the ball.
Then speed lines on our backs, and then her own head
went wobbly as a spinning egg. She'd once tracked
planetary orbits for NASA and now sat sidelined
       by her eyes' projections.

Only Bill had game.
Catatonic Bill whose normal talent was to schlub
days in a tub chair—his pudding face scarred
with chicken pox—using his hand for an ashtray,
belly for an armrest. Now all that peeled away, and he
       emerged, clean as an egg.

He was a lithe
and licorice boy, eeling past all comers, each shot
sheer net. He faked both ways, went left. Beneath the orange
rim his midair pirouettes defied the gravity that I
could barely sludge through. He scored beyond what even
       Claire could count,

then he bent panting,
hands on knees as the orderlies held out water cups,
and the rest of us reached to pat his back or slap
his sweaty hand, no one minding about the stench or his
breath like old pennies. Then as quick as that
       he went.

Inside his head
some inner winch did reel him back from the front
of his face bones where he'd been ablaze. He went back and
back into that shadowed stare. Lucky we were to breathe
his air. Breath is God's intent to keep us living. He was
       the self I'd come in

wanting to kill, and I left him there.

MARY KARR

PASTORAL

Like an otter, but warm,
she latched onto the shadowy tip
and I watched, diminished
by those amazing gulps. Finished
she let her head loll, eyes
unfocused and large: milk-drunk.

I liked afterwards best, lying
outside on a quilt, her new skin
spread out like meringue. I felt then
what a young man must feel
with his first love asleep on his breast:
desire, and the freedom to imagine it.

RITA DOVE

WAKING WITH RUSSELL

Whatever the difference is, it all began
the day we woke up face-to-face like lovers
and his four-day-old smile dawned on him again,
possessed him, till it would not fall or waver;
and I pitched back not my old hard-pressed grin
but his own smile, or one I'd rediscovered.
Dear son, I was *mezzo del cammin*
and the true path was as lost to me as ever
when you cut in front and lit it as you ran.
See how the true gift never leaves the giver:
returned and redelivered, it rolled on
until the smile poured through us like a river.
How fine, I thought, this waking amongst men!
I kissed your mouth and pledged myself forever.

DON PATERSON

YOU'RE

Clownlike, happiest on your hands,
Feet to the stars, and moon-skulled,
Gilled like a fish. A common-sense
Thumbs-down on the dodo's mode.
Wrapped up in yourself like a spool,
Trawling your dark as owls do.
Mute as a turnip from the Fourth
Of July to All Fools' Day,
O high-riser, my little loaf.

Vague as fog and looked for like mail.
Farther off than Australia.
Bent-backed Atlas, our traveled prawn.
Snug as a bud and at home
Like a sprat in a pickle jug.
A creel of eels, all ripples.
Jumpy as a Mexican bean.
Right, like a well-done sum.
A clean slate, with your own face on.

SYLVIA PLATH

"I hear you are entering the ministry," the woman said down the long table, meaning no real harm. "Was it your own idea or were you poorly advised?" And the answer that she could not have heard even if I had given it was that it was not an idea at all, neither my own nor anyone else's. It was a lump in the throat. It was an itching in the feet. It was a stirring in the blood at the sound of rain. It was a sickening of the heart at the sight of misery. It was a clamoring of ghosts. It was a name which, when I wrote it out in a dream, I knew was a name worth dying for even if I was not brave enough to do the dying myself and could not even name the name for sure. Come unto me, all ye who labor and are heavy laden, and I will give you a high and driving peace. I will condemn you to death.

I pick the children up at the bottom of the mountain where the orange bus lets them off in the wind. They run for the car like leaves blowing. Not for keeps, to be sure, but at least for the time being, the world has given them back again, and whatever the world chooses to do later on, it can never so much as lay a hand on the having-beenness of this time. The past is inviolate. We are none of us safe, but everything that has happened is safe. In all the vast and empty reaches of the universe it can never be otherwise than that when the orange bus stopped with its red lights blinking, these two children were on it. Their noses were running. One of them dropped a sweater. I drove them home.

FREDERICK BUECHNER, *The Alphabet of Grace*

DANSE RUSSE

If I when my wife is sleeping
and the baby and Kathleen
are sleeping
and the sun is a flame-white disc
in silken mists
above shining trees,—
if I in my north room
dance naked, grotesquely
before my mirror
waving my shirt round my head
and singing softly to myself:
"I am lonely, lonely.
I was born to be lonely,
I am best so!"
If I admire my arms, my face,
my shoulders, flanks, buttocks
against the yellow drawn shades,—

Who shall say I am not
the happy genius of my household?

WILLIAM CARLOS WILLIAMS

SUMMER KITCHEN

In June's high light she stood at the sink
    With a glass of wine,
And listened for the bobolink,
And crushed garlic in late sunshine.

I watched her cooking, from my chair.
    She pressed her lips
Together, reached for kitchenware,
And tasted sauce from her fingertips.

"It's ready now. Come on," she said.
    "You light the candle."
We ate, and talked, and went to bed,
And slept. It was a miracle.

DONALD HALL

THE SECOND MADRIGAL

A night of love
exquisite as a
concert from old Venice
played on exquisite instruments.
Healthy as a
buttock of a little angel.
Wise as an
anthill.
Garish as air
blown into a trumpet.
Abundant as the reign
of a royal Negro couple
seated on two thrones
cast in gold.

A night of love with you,
a big baroque battle
and two victories.

ANNA SWIR

(TRANSLATED FROM THE POLISH BY
CZESŁAW MIŁOSZ AND LEONARD NATHAN)

A BRIEF FOR THE DEFENSE

Sorrow everywhere. Slaughter everywhere. If babies
are not starving someplace, they are starving
somewhere else. With flies in their nostrils.
But we enjoy our lives because that's what God wants.
Otherwise the mornings before summer dawn would not
be made so fine. The Bengal tiger would not
be fashioned so miraculously well. The poor women
at the fountain are laughing together between
the suffering they have known and the awfulness
in their future, smiling and laughing while somebody
in the village is very sick. There is laughter
every day in the terrible streets of Calcutta,
and the women laugh in the cages of Bombay.
If we deny our happiness, resist our satisfaction,
we lessen the importance of their deprivation.
We must risk delight. We can do without pleasure,
but not delight. Not enjoyment. We must have
the stubbornness to accept our gladness in the ruthless
furnace of this world. To make injustice the only
measure of our attention is to praise the Devil.
If the locomotive of the Lord runs us down,
we should give thanks that the end had magnitude.
We must admit there will be music despite everything.
We stand at the prow again of a small ship
anchored late at night in the tiny port
looking over to the sleeping island: the waterfront
is three shuttered cafés and one naked light burning.
To hear the faint sound of oars in the silence as a rowboat
comes slowly out and then goes back is truly worth
all the years of sorrow that are to come.

JACK GILBERT

TEA AT THE PALAZ OF HOON

Not less because in purple I descended
The western day through what you called
The loneliest air, not less was I myself.

What was the ointment sprinkled on my beard?
What were the hymns that buzzed beside my ears?
What was the sea whose tide swept through me there?

Out of my mind the golden ointment rained,
And my ears made the blowing hymns they heard.
I was myself the compass of that sea:

I was the world in which I walked, and what I saw
Or heard or felt came not but from myself;
And there I found myself more truly and more strange.

WALLACE STEVENS

SUSIE ASADO

Sweet sweet sweet sweet sweet tea.
     Susie Asado.
Sweet sweet sweet sweet sweet tea.
     Susie Asado.
Susie Asado which is a told tray sure.
A lean on the shoe this means slips slips hers.
When the ancient light grey is clean it is yellow, it is a silver seller.
This is a please this is a please there are the saids to jelly. These are the
    wets these say the sets to leave a crown to Incy.
Incy is short for incubus.
A pot. A pot is a beginning of a rare bit of trees. Trees tremble, the
    old vats are in bobbles, bobbles which shade and shove and render
    clean, render clean must.
     Drink pups.
Drink pups drink pups lease a sash hold, see it shine and a bobolink
    has pins. It shows a nail.
What is a nail. A nail is unison.
Sweet sweet sweet sweet sweet tea.

GERTRUDE STEIN

Everything in the world has a spirit that can be released by its sound.

OSKAR FISCHINGER TO JOHN CAGE

JOY

"Don't cry, it's only music,"
someone's voice is saying.
"No one you love is dying."

It's only music. And it was only spring,
the world's unreasoning body
run amok, like a saint's, with glory,
that overwhelmed a young girl
into unreasoning sadness.
"Crazy," she told herself,
"I should be dancing with happiness."

But it happened again. It happens
when we make bottomless love—
there follows a bottomless sadness
which is not despair
but its nameless opposite.
It has nothing to do with the passing of time.
It's not about loss. It's about
two seemingly parallel lines
suddenly coming together
inside us, in some place
that is still wilderness.
Joy, joy, the sopranos sing,
reaching for the shimmering notes
while our eyes fill with tears.

LISEL MUELLER

THE RITES FOR COUSIN VIT

Carried her unprotesting out the door.
Kicked back the casket-stand. But it can't hold her,
That stuff and satin aiming to enfold her,
The lid's contrition nor the bolts before.
Oh oh. Too much. Too much. Even now, surmise,
She rises in the sunshine. There she goes,
Back to the bars she knew and the repose
In love-rooms and the things in people's eyes.
Too vital and too squeaking. Must emerge.
Even now she does the snake-hips with a hiss,
Slops the bad wine across her shantung, talks
Of pregnancy, guitars and bridgework, walks
In parks or alleys, comes haply on the verge
Of happiness, haply hysterics. Is.

GWENDOLYN BROOKS

ONE OF THE MANY DAYS

I never saw more frogs
than once at the back of Ben Dorain.
Joseph-coated, they ambled and jumped
in the sweet marsh grass
like coloured ideas.

The river ran glass in the sun.
I waded in the jocular water
of Loch Lyon. A parcel of hinds
gave the V-sign with their ears, then
ran off and off till they were
cantering crumbs. I watched
a whole long day
release its miracles.

But clearest of all I remember
the Joseph-coated frogs
amiably ambling or
jumping into the air—like
coloured ideas
tinily considering
the huge concept of Ben Dorain.

NORMAN MACCAIG

Authentic faith is more than an echo of a tradition. It is a creative situation, an event. For God is not always silent, and man is not always blind. In every man's life there are moments when there is a lifting of the veil at the horizon of the known, opening a sight of the eternal. Each of us has at least once in his life experienced the momentous reality of God. Each of us has once caught a glimpse of the beauty, peace and power that flow through the souls of those who are devoted to Him. But such experiences or inspirations are rare events. To some people they are like shooting stars, passing and unremembered. In others they kindle a light that is never quenched. The remembrance of that experience and the loyalty to the response of that moment are the forces that sustain our faith. In this sense, *faith is faithfulness,* loyalty to an event, loyalty to our response.

ABRAHAM JOSHUA HESCHEL, *Man Is Not Alone*

THE MOOSE

for Grace Bulmer Bowers

From narrow provinces
of fish and bread and tea,
home of the long tides
where the bay leaves the sea
twice a day and takes
the herrings long rides,

where if the river
enters or retreats
in a wall of brown foam
depends on if it meets
the bay coming in,
the bay not at home;

where, silted red,
sometimes the sun sets
facing a red sea,
and others, veins the flats'
lavender, rich mud
in burning rivulets;

on red, gravelly roads,
down rows of sugar maples,
past clapboard farmhouses
and neat, clapboard churches,
bleached, ridged as clamshells,
past twin silver birches,

through late afternoon
a bus journeys west,
the windshield flashing pink,
pink glancing off of metal,
brushing the dented flank
of blue, beat-up enamel;

down hollows, up rises,
and waits, patient, while
a lone traveller gives
kisses and embraces
to seven relatives
and a collie supervises.

Goodbye to the elms,
to the farm, to the dog.
The bus starts. The light
grows richer; the fog,
shifting, salty, thin,
comes closing in.

Its cold, round crystals
form and slide and settle
in the white hens' feathers,
in gray glazed cabbages,
on the cabbage roses
and lupins like apostles;

the sweet peas cling
to their wet white string
on the whitewashed fences;
bumblebees creep
inside the foxgloves,
and evening commences.

One stop at Bass River.
Then the Economies—
Lower, Middle, Upper;
Five Islands, Five Houses,
where a woman shakes a tablecloth
out after supper.

A pale flickering. Gone.
The Tantramar marshes
and the smell of salt hay.
An iron bridge trembles
and a loose plank rattles
but doesn't give way.

On the left, a red light
swims through the dark:
a ship's port lantern.
Two rubber boots show,
illuminated, solemn.
A dog gives one bark.

A woman climbs in
with two market bags,
brisk, freckled, elderly.
"A grand night. Yes sir,
all the way to Boston."
She regards us amicably.

Moonlight as we enter
the New Brunswick woods,
hairy, scratchy, splintery;
moonlight and mist
caught in them like lamb's wool
on bushes in a pasture.

The passengers lie back.
Snores. Some long sighs.
A dreamy divagation
begins in the night,
a gentle, auditory,
slow hallucination. . . .

In the creakings and noises,
an old conversation
—not concerning us,
but recognizable, somewhere,
back in the bus:
Grandparents' voices

uninterruptedly
talking, in Eternity:
names being mentioned,
things cleared up finally;
what he said, what she said,
who got pensioned;

deaths, deaths and sicknesses;
the year he remarried;
the year (something) happened.
She died in childbirth.
That was the son lost
when the schooner foundered.

He took to drink. Yes.
She went to the bad.
When Amos began to pray
even in the store and
finally the family had
to put him away.

"Yes . . ." that peculiar
affirmative. "Yes . . ."
A sharp, indrawn breath,
half groan, half acceptance,
that means "Life's like that.
We know *it* (also death)."

Talking the way they talked
in the old featherbed,
peacefully, on and on,
dim lamplight in the hall,
down in the kitchen, the dog
tucked in her shawl.

Now, it's all right now
even to fall asleep
just as on all those nights.
—Suddenly the bus driver
stops with a jolt,
turns off his lights.

A moose has come out of
the impenetrable wood
and stands there, looms, rather,
in the middle of the road.
It approaches; it sniffs at
the bus's hot hood.

Towering, antlerless,
high as a church,
homely as a house
(or, safe as houses).
A man's voice assures us
"Perfectly harmless. . . ."

Some of the passengers
exclaim in whispers,
childishly, softly,
"Sure are big creatures."
"It's awful plain."
"Look! It's a she!"

Taking her time,
she looks the bus over,
grand, otherworldly.
Why, why do we feel
(we all feel) this sweet
sensation of joy?

"Curious creatures,"
says our quiet driver,
rolling his *r*'s.
"Look at that, would you."
Then he shifts gears.
For a moment longer,

by craning backward,
the moose can be seen
on the moonlit macadam;
then there's a dim
smell of moose, an acrid
smell of gasoline.

ELIZABETH BISHOP

BEST LAID

it's clear
the wind
won't let up
and a swim's out—
what you planned
is scotched.
forget the calls,
errands at the mall—
yr resolve's
superfluous
as a clitoris.
how miraculous
the gratuitous—
spandrels,
cathedrals.
on a sea
of necessity
let's float
wholly
unnecessary
& call
that free

MAUREEN N. MCLANE

DEAF MUTE IN THE PEAR TREE

His clumsy body is a golden fruit
pendulous in the pear tree

Blunt fingers among the multitudinous buds

Adriatic blue the sky above and through
the forking twigs

Sun ruddying tree's trunk, his trunk
his massive head thick-nobbed with burnished curls
tight-clenched in bud

(Painting by Generalić. Primitive.)

I watch him prune with silent secateurs

Boots in the crotch of branches shift their weight
heavily as oxen in a stall

Hear small inarticulate mews from his locked mouth
a kitten in a box

Pear clippings fall
                soundlessly on the ground
Spring finches sing
                soundlessly in the leaves

A stone. A stone in ears and on his tongue

Through palm and fingertip he knows the tree's
quick springtime pulse

Smells in its sap the sweet incipient pears

Pale sunlight's choppy water glistens on
his mutely snipping blades

and flags and scraps of blue
above him make regatta of the day

But when he sees his wife's foreshortened shape
sudden and silent in the grass below
uptilt its face to him

then air is kisses, kisses

stone dissolves

his locked throat finds a little door

and through it feathered joy
flies screaming like a jay

P. K. PAGE

FROM BLOSSOMS

From blossoms comes
this brown paper bag of peaches
we bought from the boy
at the bend in the road where we turned toward
signs painted *Peaches*.

From laden boughs, from hands,
from sweet fellowship in the bins,
comes nectar at the roadside, succulent
peaches we devour, dusty skin and all,
comes the familiar dust of summer, dust we eat.

O, to take what we love inside,
to carry within us an orchard, to eat
not only the skin, but the shade,
not only the sugar, but the days, to hold
the fruit in our hands, adore it, then bite into
the round jubilance of peach.

There are days we live
as if death were nowhere
in the background; from joy
to joy to joy, from wing to wing,
from blossom to blossom to
impossible blossom, to sweet impossible blossom.

LI-YOUNG LEE

Growing up in church made for a rich symbolic life. The church itself was a huge symbol, especially when it was empty. I loved sitting in the church by myself when it was empty. It was a very pregnant symbolic life—the loaves and fishes, all the stories of the Bible, and communion.

I don't attend church now because it's not pregnant for me anymore. I see formal religion as taking calcified poetic images and worshipping them for two thousand years, but the poet is making for himself or herself fresh religious images. Emily Dickinson addressed the way people worship. She said, "They worship an eclipse."

I always thought poetry was the opposite. There's eclipse, covering, and there's apocalypse, uncovering. I think poetry provides a very important service. It uncovers our deepest identity. When we read a poem, that's what we get—our deepest identity, who we are fully. Religion is a path to this uncovering, but it's not as immediate. Poetry provides a very deep, immediate service, like a church service. It is proof of contact with God, proof that contact with God is possible, and not through a middleman. Read Emily Dickinson. Through all her quarrels, she affirms this.

LI-YOUNG LEE, "THE SUBJECT IS SILENCE"

"WHO NEVER WANTED—MADDEST JOY"

Who never wanted—maddest Joy
Remains to him unknown—
The Banquet of Abstemiousness
Defaces that of Wine—

Within its reach, though yet ungrasped
Desire's perfect Goal—
No nearer—lest the Actual—
Should disenthrall thy soul—

EMILY DICKINSON

HURRAHING IN HARVEST

Summer ends now; now, barbarous in beauty, the stooks rise
Around; up above, what wind-walks! what lovely behaviour
Of silk-sack clouds! has wilder, wilful-wavier
Meal-drift moulded ever and melted across skies?

I walk, I lift up, I lift up heart, eyes,
Down all that glory in the heavens to glean our Saviour;
And, éyes, heárt, what looks, what lips yet gave you a
Rapturous love's greeting of realer, of rounder replies?

And the azurous hung hills are his world-wielding shoulder
Majestic—as a stallion stalwart, very-violet-sweet!—
These things, these things were here and but the beholder
Wanting; which two when they once meet,
The heart rears wings bold and bolder
And hurls for him, O half hurls earth for him off under his feet.

GERARD MANLEY HOPKINS

LAUNDROMAT

Casual, sudsy
social love
at the tubs

After all, ecstasy
can't be constant

LORINE NIEDECKER

LATE BEETHOVEN

> *I haven't yet known a man who*
> *loved virtue as strongly as one*
> *loves beauty.*
>
> — CONFUCIUS

Nobody knows who she was, the Immortal
Beloved. Apart from that, everything is
clear. Feathery notes rest
peacefully on the threads of the staff
like martins just come
from the Atlantic. What would I have to be
in order to speak about him, he who's still
growing. Now we are walking alone
without ghosts or banners. Long live
chaos, say our solitary mouths.
We know that he dressed carelessly,
that he was given to fits of avarice, that he wasn't
always fair to his friends.
Friends are a hundred years
late with their impeccable smiles. Who
was the Immortal Beloved? Certainly,
he loved virtue more than beauty.
But a nameless god of beauty dwelled
in him and compelled his obedience.
He improvised for hours. A few minutes
of each improvisation were noted down.
These minutes belong neither to the nineteenth
nor to the twentieth century; as if hydrochloric
acid burned a window in velvet, thus
opening a passage to even
smoother velvet, thin as
a spiderweb. Now they name

ships and perfumes after him. They don't know who
the Immortal Beloved was, otherwise
new cities and pâtés would bear her
name. But it's useless. Only velvet
growing under velvet, like a leaf hidden
safely in another leaf. Light in darkness.
Unending adagios. That's how tired freedom
breathes. Biographers argue only
over details. Why he tormented
his nephew Karl so much. Why
he walked so fast. Why he didn't go
to London. Apart from that, everything is clear.
We don't know what music is. Who speaks
in it. To whom it is addressed. Why it is
so obstinately silent. Why it circles and returns
instead of giving a straight answer
as the Gospel demands. Prophecies
were not fulfilled. The Chinese didn't reach
the Rhine. Once more, it turned out that
the real world doesn't exist, to the immense
relief of antiquaries. The secret was hidden
somewhere else, not in soldiers'
knapsacks, but in a few notebooks.
Grillparzer, he, Chopin. Generals are
cast in lead and in tinsel to
give hell's flame a moment of respite
after kilowatts of straw. Unending adagios,
but first and foremost joy, wild
joy of shape, the laughing sister of death.

ADAM ZAGAJEWSKI

(TRANSLATED FROM THE POLISH
BY RENATA GORCZYŃSKA)

I once asked [Zagajewski] if he believed in happiness . . . and he said that he does not believe in Happiness, but he does believe in Joy. Happiness is for the Declaration of Independence, a political condition, and also for the ending of movies. Joy, by contrast, is an illumination, as in Blake and Wordsworth and Rilke, a benediction, a visitation. In the twentieth century, it required nothing less than a belief in angels.

What does such an epiphany, in a taxi in jerky traffic at mid-morning with the crowds on the pavement, and with that sense of impatience and rage that a busy city can convey—what does such a visitation of delight do but confirm the reality of the soul, the redemption of experience, the affections of hope, of gratitude to the light and to the unheard music that light contains, blessing the hectic avenue as well as a railway platform in unhappy Poland, but most of all confirming a calling, to be a poet, and to have the friendship of poetry by a writer in your own time, one who believes in archaisms, with capital letters, such as Joy and Beauty? Why be a coward, like almost every critic?

DEREK WALCOTT, "THE ELEGIST"

THE NINTH SYMPHONY OF BEETHOVEN
UNDERSTOOD AT LAST AS A SEXUAL MESSAGE

A man in terror of impotence
or infertility, not knowing the difference
a man trying to tell something
howling from the climacteric
music of the entirely
isolated soul
yelling at Joy from the tunnel of ego
music without the ghost
of another person in it, music
trying to tell something the man
does not want out, would keep if he could
gagged and bound and flogged with chords of Joy
where everything is silence and the
beating of a bloody fist upon
a splintered table

ADRIENNE RICH

BIG FINISH

Now that the last shaft of sunset has collapsed
into that rubble of cloud, let's dust off
and see how bright the stars are, the disclosed
vault spinning like a discoball been drilled
smack into Polaris. My oracle's
a bullhorn for the endtimes, portending
wars and rumors of wars in the stars' course
headlong through the heavens. And even though
the astrophysicists as in chorus
to the oracle declare that all this sparkle,
every spectacular atom of it,
is a death, the expired light of bodies
that have burned themselves down to nothing,
yet they are so bright and shimmery,
and to shimmy seems their light to me,
sequins tilting into a spotlight.
Don't they move like jubilation on their wheel?
And don't they flash with brash abandon?
And if finally they should quit their spheres
and fall upon us, their apocalypse
will surely seem a shower not of wormwood
but confetti, gleeful streaking
down the sackcloth dark to pronounce our doom.
A wop bop a loo-bop, a wop-bam-boom.

KIMBERLY JOHNSON

UNRELENTING FLOOD

Black key. White key. No,
that's wrong. It's all tactile;
it's not the information
of each struck key we love,
but how the mind and leavened
heart travel by information.
Think how blind and near-
blind pianists range along
their keyboards by clambering
over notes a sighted man
would notice to leave out,
by stringing it all on one
longing, the way bee-fingered
blind, mountainous Art
Tatum did, the way we like
joy to arrive: in such
unrelenting flood the only
way we can describe it
is by music or another
beautiful abstraction,
like the ray of sunlight
in a child's drawing
running straight to a pig's ear,
tethering us all to our star.

WILLIAM MATTHEWS

64

Distance is the soul of beauty.

SIMONE WEIL, *Gravity and Grace*

MEDITATION ON A GRAPEFRUIT

To wake when all is possible
before the agitations of the day
have gripped you
            To come to the kitchen
and peel a little basketball
for breakfast
        To tear the husk
like cotton padding   a cloud of oil
misting out of its pinprick pores
clean and sharp as pepper
                To ease
each pale pink section out of its case
so carefully   without breaking
a single pearly cell
            To slide each piece
into a cold blue china bowl
the juice pooling   until the whole
fruit is divided from its skin
and only then to eat
            so sweet
                    a discipline
precisely pointless   a devout
involvement of the hands and senses
a pause   a little emptiness

each year harder to live within
each year harder to live without

CRAIG ARNOLD

How can you expect to keep your powers of hearing when you never want to listen? That God should have time for you, you seem to take as much for granted as that you cannot have time for Him.

DAG HAMMARSKJÖLD, *Markings*

The last atom of resistance to the elemental, to the glory of the elemental, is what art is. Nature conquering herself to her own glory.

MARINA TSVETAEVA, *Art in the Light of Conscience*

BLACKBIRD ÉTUDE

for Craig Arnold

The blackbird sings at
the frontier of his music.
The branch where he sat

marks the brink of doubt,
is the outpost of his realm,
edge from which to rout

encroachers with trills
and melismatic runs sur-
passing earthbound skills.

It sounds like ardor,
it sounds like joy. We are glad
here at the border

where he signs the air
with his invisible staves,
TRESPASSERS BEWARE—

song as survival—
a kind of pure music which
we cannot rival.

A. E. STALLINGS

SLIM IN ATLANTA

Down in Atlanta,
    De whitefolks got laws
For to keep all de niggers
    From laughin' outdoors.

        Hope to Gawd I may die
            If I ain't speakin' truth
        Make de niggers do deir laughin'
            In a telefoam booth.

Slim Greer hit de town
    An' de rebs got him told,—
"Dontcha laugh on de street,
    If you want to die old."

        Den dey showed him de booth
            An' a hundred shines
        In front of it, waitin'
            In double lines.

Slim thought his sides
    Would bust in two,
Yelled, "Lookout, everybody,
    I'm coming through!"

        Pulled de other man out,
            An' bust in de box,
        An' laughed four hours
            By de Georgia clocks.

Den he peeked through de door,
　An' what did he see?
Three hundred niggers there
　In misery.—

　　Some holdin' deir sides,
　　　Some holdin' deir jaws,
　　To keep from breakin'
　　　De Georgia laws.

An' Slim gave a holler,
　An' started again;
An' from three hundred throats
　Come a moan of pain.

　　An' everytime Slim
　　　Saw what was outside,
　　Got to whoopin' again
　　　Till he nearly died.

An' while de poor critters
　Was waitin' deir chance,
Slim laughed till dey sent
　Fo' de ambulance.

　　De state paid de railroad
　　　To take him away;
　　Den, things was as usural
　　　In Atlanta, Gee A.

STERLING A. BROWN

A test of what is real is that it is hard and rough. Joys are found in it, not pleasure. What is pleasant belongs to dreams.

SIMONE WEIL, *Gravity and Grace*

STATION

Days you are sick, we get dressed slow,
find our hats, and ride the train.
We pass a junkyard and the bay,
then a dark tunnel, then a dark tunnel.

You lose your hat. I find it. The train
sighs open at Burlingame,
past dark tons of scrap and water.
I carry you down the black steps.

Burlingame is the size of joy:
a race past bakeries, gold rings
in open black cases. I don't care
who sees my crooked smile

or what erases it, past the bakery,
when you tire. We ride the blades again
beside the crooked bay. You smile.
I hold you like a hole holds light.

We wear our hats and ride the knives.
They cannot fix you. They try and try.
Tunnel! Into the dark open we go.
Days you are sick, we get dressed slow.

MARIA HUMMEL

A POEM FOR THE EPIPHANY

Ach, wie anders, wie schön
Lebt der Himmel, lebt die Erde

— GOETHE

for Ellen Jacko

It snows because the door to heaven is open,
because God is tired of working
and the day needs to be left alone.
It snows because there is a widow hiding
under her mother's bed,
because the birds are resting their throats
and three wise men are offering gifts.
Because the clouds are singing
and trees have a right to exist,
because the horses of the past are returning.
They are gray and trot gently into the barn
never touching the ground.
It snows because the wind wants
to be water, because water
wants to be powder and powder wants
to seduce the eye. Because once in his life
the philosopher has to admit
to the poverty of thought.
Because the rich man cannot buy snow
and the poor man has to wear it on his eyebrows.
Because it makes the old dog think
his life has just begun. He runs
back and forth across the parking lot.

He rolls on the snow. He laps it up.
It snows because light and dark
are making love in a field where old age
has no meaning, where colors blur,
silence covers sound, sleep covers sorrow,
everything is death, everything is joy.

PABLO MEDINA

(TRANSLATED FROM THE

SPANISH BY THE AUTHOR)

All human life is most truly, it has seemed to poets, a dream; or "a stage" Shakespeare calls it. The scientist's laboratory was called in Shakespeare's time the chemical theater. The theater of events, the histrionic plots of political powers, and the theaters of war. Men return with a language of defoliation and liquid fire to silence the earth from which they came. God is the Word in Christian theology; and He is also the Silence. The word "God" becomes necessary where there is an intense feeling of presence and oneness in opposites, an awe that cannot let go of contradictory elements, of an otherness in which I am more truly "I."

ROBERT DUNCAN, *Collected Prose*

OFTEN I AM PERMITTED TO RETURN TO A MEADOW

as if it were a scene made-up by the mind,
that is not mine, but is a made place,

that is mine, it is so near to the heart,
an eternal pasture folded in all thought
so that there is a hall therein

that is a made place, created by light
wherefrom the shadows that are forms fall.

Wherefrom fall all architectures I am
I say are likenesses of the First Beloved
whose flowers are flames lit to the Lady.

She it is Queen Under The Hill
whose hosts are a disturbance of words within words
that is a field folded.

It is only a dream of the grass blowing
east against the source of the sun
in an hour before the sun's going down

whose secret we see in a children's game
of ring a round of roses told.

Often I am permitted to return to a meadow
as if it were a given property of the mind
that certain bounds hold against chaos,

that is a place of first permission,
everlasting omen of what is.

ROBERT DUNCAN

Poetry possesses the essence of what cannot be possessed; its ultimate meaning: the impossibility of all "actuality." Joy is not a poetic sentiment (though it proceeds from a sector of the lyric universe in which chance unites, in one and the same bundle, flames and fatuities). Who has ever read a song of hope which failed to inspire a sensation of discomfort, even of disgust? And how sing a presence, when the *possible* itself is shadowed with vulgarity? Between poetry and hope, complete incompatibility: hence the poet is a prey to an ardent decomposition. Who would dare to wonder how he has experienced life when it is by death that he has been alive at all? When he succumbs to the temptation of happiness—he belongs to comedy.

E. M. CIORAN, *A Short History of Decay*

WEDDING POEM

for Keith and Jen

Friends I am here to modestly report
seeing in an orchard
in my town
a goldfinch kissing
a sunflower
again and again
dangling upside down
by its tiny claws
steadying itself by snapping open
like an old-timey fan
its wings
again and again,
until, swooning, it tumbled off
and swooped back to the very same perch,
where the sunflower curled its giant
swirling of seeds
around the bird and leaned back
to admire the soft wind
nudging the bird's plumage,
and friends I could see
the points on the flower's stately crown
soften and curl inward
as it almost indiscernibly lifted
the food of its body
to the bird's nuzzling mouth
whose fervor
I could hear from

oh 20 or 30 feet away
and see from the tiny hulls
that sailed from their
good racket,
which good racket, I have to say
was making me blush,
and rock up on my tippy-toes,
and just barely purse my lips
with what I realize now
was being, simply, glad,
which such love,
if we let it,
makes us feel.

ROSS GAY

ONCE IN A LIFETIME, SNOW

Winters at home brought wind,
black frost and raw
grey rain in barbed-wire fields,
but never more

until the day my uncle
rose at dawn
and stepped outside—to find
his paddocks gone,

his cattle to their hocks
in ghostly ground
and unaccustomed light
for miles around.

And he stopped short, and gazed
lit from below,
and half his wrinkles vanished
murmuring *Snow*.

A man of farm and fact
he stared to see
the facts of weather raised
to a mystery

white on the world he knew
and all he owned.
Snow? Here? he mused. I see.
High time I learned.

Here, guessing what he meant
had much to do
with that black earth dread old men
are given to,

he stooped to break the sheer
crust with delight
at finding the cold unknown
so deeply bright,

at feeling it take his prints
so softly deep,
as if it thought he knew
enough to sleep,

or else so little he
might seek to shift
its weight of wintry light
by a single drift,

perceiving this much, he scuffed
his slippered feet
and scooped a handful up
to taste, and eat

in memory of the fact
that even he
might not have seen the end
of reality . . .

Then, turning, he tiptoed in
to a bedroom, smiled,
and wakened a murmuring child
and another child.

LES MURRAY

PENTECOST

The neighbours hammered on the walls all night,
Outraged by the noise we made in bed.
Still we kept it up until by first light
We'd said everything that could be said.

Undaunted, we began to mewl and roar
As if desire had stripped itself of words.
Remember when we made those sounds before?
When we built a tower heavenwards
They were our reward for blasphemy.
And then again, two thousand years ago,
We huddled in a room in Galilee
Speaking languages we didn't know,
While amethyst uraeuses of flame
Hissed above us. We recalled the tower
And the tongues. We knew this was the same,
But love had turned the curse into a power.

See? It's something that we've always known:
Though we command the language of desire,
The voice of ecstasy is not our own.
We long to lose ourselves amid the choir
Of the salmon twilight and the mackerel sky,
The very air we take into our lungs,
And the rhododendron's cry.

And when you lick the sweat along my thigh,
Dearest, we renew the gift of tongues.

MICHAEL DONAGHY

C MAJOR

When he came down to the street after the rendezvous
the air was swirling with snow.
Winter had come
while they lay together.
The night shone white.
He walked quickly with joy.
The whole town was downhill.
The smiles passing by—
everyone was smiling behind turned-up collars.
It was free!
And all the question marks began singing of God's being.
So he thought.

A music broke out
and walked in the swirling snow
with long steps.
Everything on the way toward the note C.
A trembling compass directed at C.
One hour higher than the torments.
It was easy!
Behind turned-up collars everyone was smiling.

TOMAS TRANSTRÖMER

(TRANSLATED FROM THE

SWEDISH BY ROBIN FULTON)

TO THE SEA

You who cannot hear or cannot know
the terrible intricacies of our species, our minds,
the extent to which we have done
what we have done, & yet the depth to which
we have loved
what we have
loved—

the hillside
at dawn, dark eyes
outlined with the dark
sentences of kohl,
the fūl we shared
beneath the lime tree at the general's house
after visiting Goitom in prison for trying to leave
the country (the first time),
the apricot color of camels racing
on the floor of the world
as the fires blazed in celebration of Independence.

How dare I move into the dark space of your body
carrying my dreams, without an invitation, my dreams
wandering in ellipses, pet goats or chickens
devouring your yard & shirts.

Sea, my oblivious afterworld,
grant us entry, please, when we knock,
but do not keep us there, deliver
our flowers & himbasha bread.

Though we can't imagine, now, what
our dead might need,
& above all can't imagine it is over
& that they are, in fact, askless, are
needless, in fact, still hold somewhere
the smell of coffee smoking
in the house, please,
the memory of joy
fluttering like a curtain in an open window
somewhere inside the brain's secret luster
where a woman, hands red with henna,
beats the carpet clean with the stick of a broom
& the children, in the distance, choose stones
for the competition of stones, & the summer
wears a crown of beles in her green hair & the tigadelti's
white teeth & the beautiful bones of Massawa,
the gaping eyes & mouths of its arches
worn clean by the sea, your breath & your salt.
              Please, you,
being water too,
find a way into the air & then
the river & the spring
so that your waters can wash the elders,
with the medicine of the dreaming of their children,
cold & clean.

ARACELIS GIRMAY

PLUMBING

Plumbing is so intimate.
He hooks up your toilet.
He places a wax ring
under the vitreous seat
where your shit will go.
You are grateful to him.
He is a god with wrenches;
a quiet young man
using a flame torch.
He solders the joints.
He crawls through your dusty attic
over the boxes of doll furniture,
the trains, the ripped
sleeping bags, the Beatles posters,
the camp cots, the dishes, the bed springs,
to wire up the hot water tank.
And you admire him
as you would Saint Francis,
for his simple acceptance
of how things are.
And the water comes like a miracle.
Each time in the night
with your bladder full,
you rise from the bed.
And instead of the awful stench
of the day before and perhaps
even the day before that,
in a moment of pure joy
you smell nothing but the sweet

mold of an old house
and your own urine as it sloshes
down with the flush.
And you feel comfortable, taken care of,
like some rich Roman matron
who had just been loved by a boy.

RUTH STONE

THE JOY OF WRITING

Why does this written doe bound through these written woods?
For a drink of written water from a spring
whose surface will xerox her soft muzzle?
Why does she lift her head; does she hear something?
Perched on four slim legs borrowed from the truth,
she pricks up her ears beneath my fingertips.
Silence—this word also rustles across the page
and parts the boughs
that have sprouted from the word "woods."

Lying in wait, set to pounce on the blank page,
are letters up to no good,
clutches of clauses so subordinate
they'll never let her get away.

Each drop of ink contains a fair supply
of hunters, equipped with squinting eyes behind their sights,
prepared to swarm the sloping pen at any moment,
surround the doe, and slowly aim their guns.

They forget that what's here isn't life.
Other laws, black on white, obtain.
The twinkling of an eye will take as long as I say,
and will, if I wish, divide into tiny eternities,
full of bullets stopped in mid-flight.
Not a thing will ever happen unless I say so.
Without my blessing, not a leaf will fall,
not a blade of grass will bend beneath that little hoof's full stop.

Is there then a world
where I rule absolutely on fate?
A time I bind with chains of signs?
An existence become endless at my bidding?

The joy of writing.
The power of preserving.
Revenge of a mortal hand.

WISŁAWA SZYMBORSKA

(TRANSLATED FROM THE POLISH

BY CLARE CAVANAGH AND STANISŁAW BARAŃCZAK)

MEETING POINT

Time was away and somewhere else,
There were two glasses and two chairs
And two people with the one pulse
(Somebody stopped the moving stairs):
Time was away and somewhere else.

And they were neither up nor down;
The stream's music did not stop
Flowing through heather, limpid brown,
Although they sat in a coffee shop
And they were neither up nor down.

The bell was silent in the air
Holding its inverted poise—
Between the clang and clang a flower,
A brazen calyx of no noise:
The bell was silent in the air.

The camels crossed the miles of sand
That stretched around the cups and plates;
The desert was their own, they planned
To portion out the stars and dates:
The camels crossed the miles of sand.

Time was away and somewhere else.
The waiter did not come, the clock
Forgot them and the radio waltz
Came out like water from a rock:
Time was away and somewhere else.

Her fingers flicked away the ash
That bloomed again in tropic trees:
Not caring if the markets crash
When they had forests such as these,
Her fingers flicked away the ash.

God or whatever means the Good
Be praised that time can stop like this,
That what the heart has understood
Can verify in the body's peace
God or whatever means the Good.

Time was away and she was here
And life no longer what it was,
The bell was silent in the air
And all the room one glow because
Time was away and she was here.

LOUIS MACNEICE

COMING

is the body's way
of weeping, after a series
of shocks is suffered, after the thrust
of things, the gist of things, becomes
apparent: the bolt is felt completely
swollen in vicinity to wrench,
the skid is clearly headed
toward an all-out insult, and the senses
one by one abandon all their stations—
into smaller hours and thinner
minutes, seconds
split—til POW—

you had it, had it coming, and it heaved, whose participle
wasn't heaven.
That
was that.
And when you got

some senses back,
you asked yourself, is this
a dignified being's way
of being born? What
a thought
somebody had! (or some no-body)

out of the breathless blue, making us
double up like this, half gifted and
half robbed. "Rise up to me," the spirit

laughed. "I'm
coming, I'm coming,"
the body sobbed.

HEATHER MCHUGH

I would argue that the poet as well as the nonsense writer is delighted by his work, whatever the apparent extremity he may be describing in a poem. Could Hopkins, for example, have been anything but delighted/released by the phrase "time's eunuch"? Somehow he created an atomic broth (cooked over despair) that twisted these unlikely word partners together into a supremely powerful and economical description of supreme powerlessness and waste. He is, in the moment of calling himself "time's eunuch," released from *being* "time's eunuch." I wouldn't be at all surprised if he actually laughed. I don't think it would be a rueful laugh, either; it would be joy.

KAY RYAN, "A CONSIDERATION OF POETRY"

TRUE LOVE

In the middle of the night, when we get up
after making love, we look at each other in
complete friendship, we know so fully
what the other has been doing. Bound to each other
like mountaineers coming down from a mountain,
bound with the tie of the delivery room,
we wander down the hall to the bathroom, I can
hardly walk, I wobble through the granular
shadowless air, I know where you are
with my eyes closed, we are bound to each other
with huge invisible threads, our sexes
muted, exhausted, crushed, the whole
body a sex—surely this
is the most blessed time of my life,
our children asleep in their beds, each fate
like a vein of abiding mineral
not discovered yet. I sit
on the toilet in the night, you are somewhere in the room,
I open the window and snow has fallen in a
steep drift, against the pane, I
look up, into it,
a wall of cold crystals, silent
and glistening, I quietly call to you
and you come and hold my hand and I say
I cannot see beyond it. I cannot see beyond it.

SHARON OLDS

ONCE, I

Once, I
was seven Spanish bullocks in a high meadow,
sleepy and nameless.

As-ifness strange to myself, but complete.

Light on the neck-nape
of time
as two wings of one starling,

or lovers so happy
neither needs think of the other.

JANE HIRSHFIELD

TRACTOR

The tractor stands frozen—an agony
To think of. All night
Snow packed its open entrails. Now a head-pincering gale,
A spill of molten ice, smoking snow,
Pours into its steel.
At white heat of numbness it stands
In the aimed hosing of ground-level fieriness.

It defies flesh and won't start.
Hands are like wounds already
Inside armour gloves, and feet are unbelievable
As if the toe-nails were all just torn off.
I stare at it in hatred. Beyond it
The copse hisses—capitulates miserably
In the fleeing, failing light. Starlings,
A dirtier sleetier snow, blow smokily, unendingly, over
Towards plantations eastward.
All the time the tractor is sinking
Through the degrees, deepening
Into its hell of ice.

The starting lever
Cracks its action, like a snapping knuckle.
The battery is alive—but like a lamb
Trying to nudge its solid-frozen mother—
While the seat claims my buttock-bones, bites
With the space-cold of earth, which it has joined
In one solid lump.

I squirt commercial sure-fire
Down the black throat—it just coughs.
It ridicules me—a trap of iron stupidity
I've stepped into. I drive the battery
As if I were hammering and hammering
The frozen arrangement to pieces with a hammer
And it jabbers laughing pain-crying mockingly
Into happy life.

And stands
Shuddering itself full of heat, seeming to enlarge slowly
Like a demon demonstrating
A more-than-usually-complete materialization—
Suddenly it jerks from its solidarity
With the concrete, and lurches towards a stanchion
Bursting with superhuman well-being and abandon
Shouting Where Where?

Worse iron is waiting. Power-lift kneels,
Levers awake imprisoned deadweight,
Shackle-pins bedded in cast-iron cow-shit.
The blind and vibrating condemned obedience
Of iron to the cruelty of iron,
Wheels screeched out of their night-locks—

Fingers
Among the tormented
Tonnage and burning of iron

Eyes
Weeping in the wind of chloroform

And the tractor, streaming with sweat,
Raging and trembling and rejoicing.

TED HUGHES

I think of poems as a sort of animal. They have their own life, like animals, by which I mean that they seem quite separate from any person, even from their author, and nothing can be added to them or taken away without maiming and perhaps even killing them. And they have a certain wisdom. They know something special . . . something perhaps which we are very curious to learn. Maybe my concern has been to capture not animals particularly and not poems, but simply things which have a vivid life of their own outside mine.

TED HUGHES, *Winter Pollen*

In my childhood, when the presence of God seemed everywhere and I seemed to myself a mote of exception, improbable as a flaw in the sun, the very sweetness of the experience lay in that stinging thought—not me, not like me, not mine.

MARILYNNE ROBINSON, *The Death of Adam*

YOKO

All today I lie in the bottom of the wardrobe
feeling low but sometimes getting up
to moodily lumber across rooms
and lap from the toilet bowl, it is so sultry
and then I hear the noise of firecrackers again
all New York is jaggedy with firecrackers today
and I go back to the wardrobe gloomy
trying to void my mind of them.
I am confused, I feel loose and unfitted.

At last deep in the stairwell I hear a tread,
it is him, my leader, my love.
I run to the door and listen to his approach.
Now I can smell him, what a good man he is,
I love it when he has the sweat of work on him,
as he enters I yodel with happiness,
I throw my body up against his, I try to lick his lips,
I care about him more than anything.

After we eat we go for a walk to the piers.
I leap into the standing warmth, I plunge into
the combination of old and new smells.
Here on a garbage can at the bottom, so interesting,
what sister or brother I wonder left this message I sniff.
I too piss there, and go on.
Here a hydrant there a pole
here's a smell I left yesterday, well that's disappointing
but I piss there anyway, and go on.

I investigate so much that in the end
it is for form's sake only, only a drop comes out.

I investigate tar and rotten sandwiches, everything, and go on.

And here a dried old turd, so interesting
so old, so dry, yet so subtle and mellow.
I can place it finely, I really appreciate it,
a gold distant smell like packed autumn leaves in winter
reminding me how what is rich and fierce when excreted
becomes weathered and mild
                              but always interesting
and reminding me of what I have to do.

My leader looks on and expresses his approval.

I sniff it well and later I sniff the air well
a wind is meeting us after the close July day
rain is getting near too but first the wind.

Joy, joy,
being outside with you, active, investigating it all,
with bowels emptied, feeling your approval
and then running on, the big fleet Yoko,
my body in its excellent black coat never lets me down,
returning to you (as I always will, you know that)
and now
                   filling myself out with myself, no longer confused,
my panting pushing apart my black lips, but unmoving,
I stand with you braced against the wind.

THOM GUNN

For some months now I have lived with my own youth and child-hood, not always writing indeed but thinking of it almost every day, and I am sorrowful and disturbed. It is not that I have accomplished too few of my plans, for I am not ambitious; but when I think of all the books I have read, and of the wise words I have heard spoken, and of the anxiety I have given to parents and grandparents, and of the hopes that I have had, all life weighed in the scales of my own life seems to me a preparation for something that never happens.

W. B. YEATS, *Autobiographies*

from VACILLATION

My fiftieth year had come and gone,
I sat, a solitary man,
In a crowded London shop,
An open book and empty cup
On the marble table-top.

While on the shop and street I gazed
My body of a sudden blazed;
And twenty minutes more or less
It seemed, so great my happiness,
That I was blessèd and could bless.

W. B. YEATS

MEMOIR

Orwell says somewhere that no one ever writes the real story of
    their life.
The real story of a life is the story of its humiliations.
If I wrote that story now—
radioactive to the end of time—
people, I swear, your eyes would fall out, you couldn't peel
the gloves fast enough
from your hands scorched by the firestorms of that shame.
Your poor hands. Your poor eyes
to see me weeping in my room
or boring the tall blonde to death.
Once I accused the innocent.
Once I bowed and prayed to the guilty.
I still wince at what I once said to the devastated widow.
And one October afternoon, under a locust tree
whose blackened pods were falling and making
illuminating patterns on the pathway,
I was seized by joy,
and someone saw me there,
and that was the worst of all,
lacerating and unforgettable.

VIJAY SESHADRI

THE RAPTURE OF DRY ICE BURNING OFF SKIN
AS THE MOMENT OF THE SOUL'S APOTHEOSIS

How will we get used to joy
if we won't hold onto it?

Not even extinction stops me; when
I've sufficient craving, I follow the buffalo,
their hair hanging below their stomachs like
fringes on Tiffany lampshades; they can be turned on
so can I by a stampede, footsteps whose sound
is my heart souped up, doctored, ninety pounds
running off a semi's invincible engine. Buffalo
heaven is Niagara Falls. There their spirit
gushes. There they still stampede and power
the generators that operate the Tiffany lamps
that let us see in some of the dark. Snow
inundates the city bearing their name; buffalo
spirit chips later melt to feed the underground,
the politically dredlocked tendrils of roots. And this
has no place in reality, is trivial juxtaposed with

the faces of addicts, their eyes practically as sunken
as extinction, gray ripples like hurdlers' track lanes
under them, pupils like just more needle sites.
And their arms: flesh trying for a moon apprenticeship,
a celestial antibody. Every time I use it
the umbrella is turned inside out,
metal veins, totally hardened arteries and survival
without anything flowing within, nothing saying
life came from the sea, from anywhere but coincidence
or God's ulcer, revealed. Yet also, inside out

the umbrella tries to be a bouquet, or at least
the rugged wrapping for one that must endure much,
without dispensing coherent parcels of scent,
before the refuge of vase in a room already accustomed
to withering mind and retreating skin. But the smell
of the flowers lifts the corners of the mouth as if
the man at the center of this remorse has lifted her
in a waltz. This is as true as sickness. The Jehovah's

Witness will come to my door any minute with tracts, an
inflexible agenda and I won't let him in because
I'm painting a rosy picture with only blue and
yellow (sadness and cowardice).
I'm something of an alchemist. Extinct.
He would tell me time is running out.
I would correct him: time *ran* out; that's why
history repeats itself, why we can't advance.
What joy will come has to be here right now: Cheer
to wash the dirt away, Twenty Mule Team Borax and
Arm & Hammer to magnify Cheer's power, lemon-scented
bleach and ammonia to trick the nose, improved—changed—
Tide, almost all-purpose starch that cures any limpness
except impotence. Celebrate that there's *Master*card
to rule us, bring us to our knees, the protocol we follow
in the presence of the head of our state of ruin, the
official with us all the time, not inaccessible in
palaces or White Houses or Kremlins. Besides every
ritual is stylized, has patterns and repetitions

suitable for adaptation to dance. Here come toe shoes,
brushstrokes, oxymorons. Joy

is at our tongue tips: let the great thirsts and hungers
of the world be the *marvelous* thirsts, *glorious* hungers.
Let heartbreak be alternative to coffeebreak, five
midmorning minutes devoted to emotion.

THYLIAS MOSS

AND I WAS ALIVE

And I was alive in the blizzard of the blossoming pear,
Myself I stood in the storm of the bird-cherry tree.
It was all leaflife and starshower, unerring, self-shattering
      power,
And it was all aimed at me.

What is this dire delight flowering fleeing always earth?
What is being? What is truth?

Blossoms rupture and rapture the air,
All hover and hammer,
Time intensified and time intolerable, sweetness raveling rot.
It is now. It is not.

OSIP MANDELSTAM

(TRANSLATED FROM THE RUSSIAN

BY CHRISTIAN WIMAN)

I have never known a man who lived so greedily for the passing hours as M. He seemed to have an almost physical sense of time, of the minutes which compose it. In this respect he was the exact opposite of Berdiayev, who says somewhere that he could never abide time and that all the anguish of waiting is longing for eternity. It seems to me that for any artist eternity is something tangibly present in every fleeting fraction of time, which he would gladly stop and thus make even more tangible. What causes anguish in an artist is not longing for eternity, but a temporary loss of his feeling that every second of time is, in its fullness and density, the equal of eternity itself.

NADEZHDA MANDELSTAM, *Hope Against Hope*

To exist is the artist's greatest pride. He desires no paradise other than being.

OSIP MANDELSTAM, "THE MORNING OF ACMEISM"

There is always an enormous temptation in all of life to diddle around making itsy-bitsy friends and meals and journeys for itsy-bitsy years on end. It is so self-conscious, so apparently moral, simply to step aside from the gaps where the creeks and winds pour down, saying, I never merited this grace, quite rightly, and then to sulk along the rest of your days on the edge of rage. I won't have it. The world is wilder than that in all directions, more dangerous and bitter, more extravagant and bright. We are making hay when we should be making whoopee; we are raising tomatoes when we should be raising Cain, or Lazarus.

ANNIE DILLARD, *Pilgrim at Tinker Creek*

LITTLE CLOWN, MY HEART

Little clown, my heart
Spangled again and lopsided,
Handstands and Peking pirouettes,
Backflips snapping open like
A carpenter's hinged ruler,

Little gimp-footed hurray,
Paper parasol of pleasures,
Fleshy undertongue of sorrows,
Sweet potato plant of my addictions,

Acapulco cliff-diver *corazón,*
Fine as an obsidian dagger,
Alley-oop and here we go
Into the froth, my life,
Into the flames!

SANDRA CISNEROS

LAND'S END

This air,
you say, *feels as if it hasn't touched land*
for a thousand miles,

as surf sound washes through scrub
and eucalyptus,
whether ocean or wind in the trees

or both: the park's big windmill
turning overhead
while joggers circle the ball field

only a few yards off
this path secreted in growth and mist,
the feel of a long narrow theater set

about it here on the park's western edge
just in from the highway
then the moody swells of the Pacific.

The way the chill goes out of us
and the sweat comes up
as we drive back into the heat

and how I need to take you
to all the special places, or show
you where the fog rolls down

and breaks apart in these hills or where
that gorgeous little piano bridge
comes halfway through the song,

because when what has become dormant,
meager or hardened
passes through the electric

of you, the fugitive scattered pieces
are called back to their nature—
light pouring through muslin

in a strange, bare room.

AUGUST KLEINZAHLER

These moments are immortal, and most transitory of all; no content may be secured from them. . . . Beams of their power stream into the ordered world and dissolve it again and again.

MARTIN BUBER, I and Thou

"In order to come to love," says Kierkegaard about his renunciation of Regina Olsen, "I had to remove the object." That is sublimely to misunderstand God. Creation is not a hurdle on the road to God, it is the road itself.

MARTIN BUBER, Between Man and Man

PROCEDURE

This tea, this cup of tea, made of leaves,
made of the leaves of herbs and absolute

almond blossom, this tea, is the interpreter
of almond, liquid touchstone which lets us
scent its true taste at last and with a bump,

in my case, takes me back to the yellow time
of trouble with blood tests, and cellular
madness, and my presence required

on the slab for the surgery, and all that mess
I don't want to comb through here because
it seems, honestly, a trifle now that steam

and scent and strength and steep and infusion
say thank you thank you thank you for the then, and now

JO SHAPCOTT

ODE TO THE URGE

Urination is the major accomplishment of engineering
at least insofar as drainage is concerned.
Furthermore, to urinate is a pleasure.
What's there to say? One takes a leak
saluting love and friends,
one spills himself long into the throat of the world
to remind himself we're warm inside, and to stay tuned up.
All this is important
now that the world's emitting disaster signals,
intoxicated hiccups.
Because it's necessary, for pure love of life, to urinate
on the silver service,
on the seats of sports cars,
in swimming pools with underwater lights
worth easily 15 or 16 times more than their owners.
To urinate until our throats ache,
right down to the last drops of blood.
To urinate on those who see life as a waltz,
to scream at them, Long live the Cumbia, señores,
Everybody up to shake his ass,
until we shake off this mystery we are
and the fucked-up love of suffering it.
And long live the Jarabe Zapateado too,
because reality is in the back and to the right,
where you don't go wearing a tux.
(Nobody's yet gotten rid of TB by beating his chest.)
I'm pissing down from the manger of life:
I just want to be the greatest pisser in history,
Oh Mama, for the love of God, the greatest pisser in history.

RICARDO CASTILLO

(TRANSLATED FROM THE SPANISH BY ROBERT L. JONES)

LORE

Job Davies, eighty-five
Winters old, and still alive
After the slow poison
And treachery of the seasons.

Miserable? Kick my arse!
It needs more than the rain's hearse,
Wind-drawn, to pull me off
The great perch of my laugh.

What's living but courage?
Paunch full of hot porridge,
Nerves strengthened with tea,
Peat-black, dawn found me

Mowing where the grass grew,
Bearded with golden dew.
Rhythm of the long scythe
Kept this tall frame lithe.

What to do? Stay green.
Never mind the machine,
Whose fuel is human souls.
Live large, man, and dream small.

R. S. THOMAS

from POEMS FOR MOSCOW

From my hands—take this city not made by hands,
my strange, my beautiful brother.

Take it, church by church—all forty times forty churches,
and flying up the roofs, the small pigeons;

And Spassky Gates—and gates, and gates—
where the Orthodox take off their hats;

And the Chapel of Stars—refuge chapel—
where the floor is—polished by tears;

Take the circle of the five cathedrals,
my coal, my soul; the domes wash us in their darkgold,

And on your shoulders, from the red clouds,
the Mother of God will drop her own thin coat,

And you will rise, happened of wonderpowers
—never ashamed you loved me.

MARINA TSVETAEVA

(TRANSLATED FROM THE RUSSIAN

BY ILYA KAMINSKY AND JEAN VALENTINE)

THE SEASON OF PHANTASMAL PEACE

Then all the nations of birds lifted together
the huge net of the shadows of this earth
in multitudinous dialects, twittering tongues,
stitching and crossing it. They lifted up
the shadows of long pines down trackless slopes,
the shadows of glass-faced towers down evening streets,
the shadow of a frail plant on a city sill—
the net rising soundless as night, the birds' cries soundless, until
there was no longer dusk, or season, decline, or weather,
only this passage of phantasmal light
that not the narrowest shadow dared to sever.

And men could not see, looking up, what the wild geese drew,
what the ospreys trailed behind them in silvery ropes
that flashed in the icy sunlight; they could not hear
battalions of starlings waging peaceful cries,
bearing the net higher, covering this world
like the vines of an orchard, or a mother drawing
the trembling gauze over the trembling eyes
of a child fluttering to sleep;
                                        it was the light
that you will see at evening on the side of a hill
in yellow October, and no one hearing knew
what change had brought into the raven's cawing,
the killdeer's screech, the ember-circling chough
such an immense, soundless, and high concern
for the fields and cities where the birds belong,
except it was their seasonal passing, Love,
made seasonless, or, from the high privilege of their birth,

something brighter than pity for the wingless ones
below them who shared dark holes in windows and in houses,
and higher they lifted the net with soundless voices
above all change, betrayals of falling suns,
and this season lasted one moment, like the pause
between dusk and darkness, between fury and peace,
but, for such as our earth is now, it lasted long.

DEREK WALCOTT

BUT I, TOO, WANT TO BE A POET

But I, too, want to be a poet
to erase from my days
confusion & poverty
fiction & a sharp tongue

To sing again
with the tones of adolescence
demanding vengeance
against my enemies, with words
clear & austere

To end this tumultuous quest
for reasonable solutions
to situations mysterious & sore

To have the height to view
myself as I view others
with lenience & love

To be free of the need
to make a waste of money
when my passion,
first and last,
is for the ecstatic lash
of the poetic line

and no visible recompense

FANNY HOWE

When I don't understand a poem, or part of it, I don't insist: I try
to be satisfied with what I understand, and I'm sure that another
time, under other conditions, I'll understand more and understand
something else . . . the understanding of a poem comes in successive
surprises.

There is a place within us that can be reached by intelligence. But
there is a deeper one that only the spirit can get to. And that is why
those who are "merely completely intelligent"—in science or art,
verse or prose—always seem like spies.

The world does not need to come from a god. For better or worse,
the world is here. But it does need to *go* to one (where is he?), and
that is why the poet exists.

JUAN RAMÓN JIMÉNEZ, The Complete Perfectionist

DAWN OUTSIDE THE CITY WALLS

You can see the face of everything, and it is white—
plaster, nightmare, adobe, anemia, cold—
turned to the east. Oh closeness to life!
Hardness of life! Like something
in the body that is animal—root, slag-ends—
with the soul still not set well there—
and mineral and vegetable!
Sun standing stiffly against man,
against the sow, the cabbages, the mud wall!
—False joy, because you are merely
in time, as they say, and not in the soul!

    The entire sky taken up
by moist and steaming heaps,
a horizon of dung piles.
Sour remains, here and there,
of the night. Slices
of the green moon, half-eaten,
crystal bits from false stars,
plaster, the paper ripped off, still faintly
sky-blue. The birds
not really awake yet, in the raw moon,
streetlight nearly out.
Mob of beings and things!
—A true sadness, because you are really deep
in the soul, as they say, not in time at all!

JUAN RAMÓN JIMÉNEZ
(TRANSLATED FROM THE
SPANISH BY ROBERT BLY)

THE ACHE OF MARRIAGE

The ache of marriage:

thigh and tongue, beloved,
are heavy with it,
it throbs in the teeth

We look for communion
and are turned away, beloved,
each and each

It is leviathan and we
in its belly
looking for joy, some joy
not to be known outside it

two by two in the ark of
the ache of it.

DENISE LEVERTOV

Real love came much later. It lay at the end of a long and arduous road, and up to the very last moment I had been convinced it wouldn't happen. I was so surprised by its arrival, so unprepared, that on the day it arrived I had already arranged for us to visit the Holocaust museum at Auschwitz. You were holding my feet on the train to the bus that would take us there. We were heading toward all that makes life intolerable, feeling the only thing that makes it worthwhile. That was joy. But it's no good thinking about or discussing it. It has no place next to the furious argument about who cleaned the house or picked up the child. It is irrelevant when sitting peacefully, watching an old movie, or doing an impression of two old ladies in a shop, or as I eat a popsicle while you scowl at me, or when working on different floors of the library. It doesn't fit with the everyday. The thing no one ever tells you about joy is that it has very little real pleasure in it. And yet if it hadn't happened at all, at least once, how would we live?

ZADIE SMITH, "JOY"

HAPPINESS

I have been taught never to brag but now
I cannot help it: I keep
a beautiful garden, all abundance,
indiscriminate, pulling itself
from the stubborn earth: does it offend you
to watch me working in it,
touching my hands to the greening tips or
tearing the yellow stalks back, so wild
the living and the dead both
snap off in my hands?
The neighbor with his stuttering
fingers, the neighbor with his broken
love: each comes up my drive
to receive his pitying,
accustomed consolations, watches me
work in silence awhile, rises in anger,
walks back. Does it offend them to watch me
not mourning with them but working
fitfully, fruitlessly, working
the way the bees work, which is to say
by instinct alone, which looks like pleasure?
I can stand for hours among the sweet
narcissus, silent as a point of bone.
I can wait longer than sadness. I can wait longer
than your grief. It is such a small thing
to be proud of, a garden. Today
there were scrub jays, quail,
a woodpecker knocking at the white-
and-black shapes of trees, and someone's lost rabbit

scratching under the barberry: is it
indiscriminate? Should it shrink back, wither,
and expurgate? Should I, too, not be loved?
It is only a little time, a little space.
Why not watch the grasses take up their colors in a rush
like a stream of kerosene being lit?
If I could not have made this garden beautiful
I wouldn't understand your suffering,
nor care for each the same, inflamed way.
I would have to stay only like the bees,
beyond consciousness, beyond
self-reproach, fingers dug down hard
into stone, and growing nothing.
There is no end to ego,
with its museum of disappointments.
I want to take my neighbors into the garden
and show them: Here is consolation.
Here is your pity. Look how much seed it drops
around the sparrows as they fight.
It lives alongside their misery.
It glows each evening with a violent light.

PAISLEY REKDAL

ACCIDENTS OF BIRTH

> Je vois les effroyables espaces de
> l'Univers qui m'enferment, et je
> me trouve attaché à un coin de
> cette vaste étendue, sans savoir
> pourquoi je suis plutôt en ce lieu
> qu'en un autre, ni pourquoi ce peu
> de temps qui m'est donné à vivre
> m'est assigné à ce point plutôt qu'à
> un autre de toute l'éternité qui m'a
> précédé, et de toute qui me suit.
>
> —PASCAL, *Pensées sur la religion*

> *The approach of a man's life out*
> *of the past is history, and the*
> *approach of time out of the future*
> *is mystery. Their meeting is the*
> *present, and it is consciousness, the*
> *only time life is alive. The endless*
> *wonder of this meeting is what*
> *causes the mind, in its inward lib-*
> *erty of a frozen morning, to turn*
> *back and question and remember.*
> *The world is full of places. Why is*
> *it that I am here?*
>
> —WENDELL BERRY, *The Long-Legged House*

Spared by a car- or airplane-crash or
cured of malignancy, people look
around with new eyes at a newly
praiseworthy world, blinking eyes like these.

For I've been brought back again from the
fine silt, the mud where our atoms lie
down for long naps. And I've also been
pardoned miraculously for years
by the lava of chance which runs down
the world's gullies, silting us back.
Here I am, brought back, set up, not yet happened away.

But it's not this random
life only, throwing its sensual
astonishments upside down on
the bloody membranes behind my eyeballs,
not just me being here again, old
needer, looking for someone to need,
but you, up from the clay yourself,
as luck would have it, and inching
over the same little segment of earth-
ball, in the same little eon, to
meet in a room, alive in our skins,
and the whole galaxy gaping there
and the centuries whining like gnats—
you, to teach me to see it, to see
it with you, and to offer somebody
uncomprehending, impudent thanks.

WILLIAM MEREDITH

FAR FROM KINGDOMS

Far from kingdoms
how steady is the room!
Come, breathe close with me
so I may discover the sweetness
of many imperfections, some missing
tooth, some extra wrinkle, and your body
worn out slightly by carelessness.

PATRIZIA CAVALLI

(TRANSLATED FROM THE ITALIAN

BY JUDITH BAUMEL)

I'D RATHER GO WITH YOU

I'd rather go with you and mince precisely
through whoop-cream worlds
sugar-belled by kissy-buds
down aisles brailled with frippery—

Let's go galloping, Lieblings,
with the nimbleness of minks across
our circumstance of ice

And like old hippies skinny-dipping
up past the beaver dam
where Dad and I honeymooned
back when autumn hydrangeas greened,
never speak of slipping.

In the Chinatown of childhood
a ten-foot-tall deal dresser's hundred drawers
wink open one by one on the miraculous—

We'll make it there, my little livers
and when we do I swear
I shan't be penurious.

DANIELLE CHAPMAN

COMING

On longer evenings,
Light, chill and yellow,
Bathes the serene
Foreheads of houses.
A thrush sings,
Laurel-surrounded
In the deep bare garden,
Its fresh-peeled voice
Astonishing the brickwork.
It will be spring soon,
It will be spring soon—
And I, whose childhood
Is a forgotten boredom,
Feel like a child
Who comes on a scene
Of adult reconciling,
And can understand nothing
But the unusual laughter,
And starts to be happy.

PHILIP LARKIN

In those days boredom for me was a misery and a passion, and anticipation a pleasure so sharp I could not tell it from dread. . . . I do not remember childhood as happy but as filled and overfilled with an intensity of experience that made happiness a matter of little interest.

MARILYNNE ROBINSON, *The Death of Adam*

KING DAVID DANCES

Aware to the dry throat of the wide hell in the world
O trampling empires, and mine one of them,
and mine one gross desire against His sight,
slaughter devising there,
some good behind, ambiguous ahead,
revolted sons, a pierced son, bound to bear,
mid hypocrites amongst idolaters,
mockt in abysm by one shallow wife,
with the ponder both of priesthood & of State
heavy upon me, yea,
all the black same I dance my blue head off!

JOHN BERRYMAN

THE ANSWER

When I go back to earth
And all my joyous body
Puts off the red and white
That once had been so proud,
If men should pass above
With false and feeble pity,
My dust will find a voice
To answer them aloud:

"Be still, I am content,
Take back your poor compassion!—
Joy was a flame in me
Too steady to destroy.
Lithe as a bending reed
Loving the storm that sways her—
I found more joy in sorrow
Than you could find in joy."

SARA TEASDALE

EPITAPH

So I may say,
"I died of living,
having lived one hour";

so they may say,
"she died soliciting
illicit fervour";

so you may say,
"Greek flower; Greek ecstasy
reclaims for ever

one who died
following
intricate songs' lost measure."

H.D.

THE LEMONS

Listen to me, the poets laureate
walk only among plants
with rare names: boxwood, privet and acanthus.
But like roads that lead to grassy
ditches where boys
scoop up a few starved
eels out of half-dry puddles:
paths that run along the banks,
come down among the tufted canes
and end in orchards, among the lemon trees.

Better if the hubbub of the birds
dies out, swallowed by the blue:
we can hear more of the whispering
of friendly branches in not-quite-quiet air,
and the sensations of this smell
that can't divorce itself from earth
and rains a restless sweetness on the heart.
Here, by some miracle, the war
of troubled passions calls a truce;
here we poor, too, receive our share of riches,
which is the fragrance of the lemons.

See, in these silences where things
give over and seem on the verge of betraying
their final secret,
sometimes we feel we're about
to uncover an error in Nature,
the still point of the world, the link that won't hold,

the thread to untangle that will finally lead
to the heart of a truth.
The eye scans its surroundings,
the mind inquires aligns divides
in the perfume that gets diffused
at the day's most languid.
It's in these silences you see
in every fleeting human
shadow some disturbed Divinity.

But the illusion fails, and time returns us
to noisy cities where the blue
is seen in patches, up between the roofs.
The rain exhausts the earth then;
winter's tedium weighs the houses down,
the light turns miserly—the soul bitter.
Till one day through a half-shut gate
in a courtyard, there among the trees,
we can see the yellow of the lemons;
and the chill in the heart
melts, and deep in us
the golden horns of sunlight
pelt their songs.

EUGENIO MONTALE

(TRANSLATED FROM THE ITALIAN

BY JONATHAN GALASSI)

The poem, for all its bounty, is a construct, and though the words in it may give the fiercest light, we cannot live there. Poems are excursions into belief and doubt, often simultaneously.

TESS GALLAGHER, "THE POEM AS TIME MACHINE"

Pietak thanked God for every poem. He scribbled his thanks on the margins of his drafts. And he was an atheist.

ANNA KAMIENSKA, "INDUSTRIOUS AMAZEMENT"

MANIFESTO: THE MAD FARMER LIBERATION FRONT

Love the quick profit, the annual raise,
vacation with pay. Want more
of everything ready-made. Be afraid
to know your neighbors and to die.
And you will have a window in your head.
Not even your future will be a mystery
any more. Your mind will be punched in a card
and shut away in a little drawer.
When they want you to buy something
they will call you. When they want you
to die for profit they will let you know.
So, friends, every day do something
that won't compute. Love the Lord.
Love the world. Work for nothing.
Take all that you have and be poor.
Love someone who does not deserve it.
Denounce the government and embrace
the flag. Hope to live in that free
republic for which it stands.
Give your approval to all you cannot
understand. Praise ignorance, for what man
has not encountered he has not destroyed.
Ask the questions that have no answers.
Invest in the millennium. Plant sequoias.
Say that your main crop is the forest
that you did not plant,
that you will not live to harvest.
Say that the leaves are harvested
when they have rotted into the mold.

Call that profit. Prophesy such returns.
Put your faith in the two inches of humus
that will build under the trees
every thousand years.
Listen to carrion—put your ear
close, and hear the faint chattering
of the songs that are to come.
Expect the end of the world. Laugh.
Laughter is immeasurable. Be joyful
though you have considered all the facts.
So long as women do not go cheap
for power, please women more than men.
Ask yourself: Will this satisfy
a woman satisfied to bear a child?
Will this disturb the sleep
of a woman near to giving birth?
Go with your love to the fields.
Lie easy in the shade. Rest your head
in her lap. Swear allegiance
to what is nighest your thoughts.
As soon as the generals and the politicos
can predict the motions of your mind,
lose it. Leave it as a sign
to mark the false trail, the way
you didn't go. Be like the fox
who makes more tracks than necessary,
some in the wrong direction.
Practice resurrection.

WENDELL BERRY

"LOVE OF MY FLESH, LIVING DEATH"

after García Lorca

Once I wasn't always so plain.
I was strewn feathers on a cross
of dune, an expanse of ocean
at my feet, garlands of gulls.

Sirens and gulls. They couldn't tame you.
You know as well as they: to be
a dove is to bear the falcon
at your breast, your nights, your seas.

My fear is simple, heart-faced
above a flare of etchings, a lineage
in letters, my sudden stare. It's you.

It's you! sang the heart upon its mantel
pelvis. Blush of my breath, catch
of my see—beautiful bird—It's you.

LORNA DEE CERVANTES

To turn from everything to one face is to find oneself face to face
with everything.

ELIZABETH BOWEN, *The Heat of the Day*

GLAMOURIE

When I found I'd lost you—
not beside me, nor ahead,
nor right nor left not
your green jacket moving

between the trees anywhere—
I waited a long while
before wandering on. No wren
jinked in the undergrowth,

not a twig snapped.
It was hardly the Wildwood—
just some auld fairmer's
shelter belt—but red haws

reached out to me,
and between fallen leaves
pretty white flowers bloomed
late into their year. I tried

calling out, or think
I did, but your name
shrivelled on my tongue,
so instead I strolled on

through the wood's good
offices, and duly fell
to wondering if I hadn't
simply made it all up. You,

I mean, everything,
my entire life. Either way,
nothing now could touch me
bar my hosts, who appeared

as diffuse golden light,
as tiny spiders
examining my hair . . .
what gratitude I felt then—

I might be gone for ages,
maybe seven years!—
and such sudden joie de vivre
that when a ditch gaped

right there instantly in front of me
I jumped it, blithe as a girl—
ach, I jumped clear over it,
without even pausing to think.

KATHLEEN JAMIE

AFTER ARGUING AGAINST THE CONTENTION THAT ART MUST COME FROM DISCONTENT

Whispering to each handhold, "I'll be back,"
I go up the cliff in the dark. One place
I loosen a rock and listen a long time
till it hits, faint in the gulf, but the rush
of the torrent almost drowns it out, and the wind—
I almost forgot the wind: it tears at your side
or it waits and then buffets; you sag outward. . . .

I remember they said it would be hard. I scramble
by luck into a little pocket out of
the wind and begin to beat on the stones
with my scratched numb hands, rocking back and forth
in silent laughter there in the dark—
"Made it again!" Oh how I love this climb!
—the whispering to stones, the drag, the weight
as your muscles crack and ease on, working
right. They are back there, discontent,
waiting to be driven forth. I pound
on the earth, riding the earth past the stars:
"Made it again! Made it again!"

WILLIAM STAFFORD

But there is not only peacefulness, there is joy. And the joy, less deniable in its evidence than the peacefulness, is the confirmation of it. I sat one summer evening and watched a great blue heron make his descent from the top of the hill into the valley. He came down at a measured deliberate pace, stately as always, like a dignitary going down a stair. And then, at a point I judged to be midway over the river, without at all varying his wingbeat he did a backward turn in the air, a loop-the-loop. It could only have been a gesture of pure exuberance, of joy—a speaking of his sense of the evening, the day's fulfillment, his descent homeward. He made just that one slow turn, and then flew on out of sight in the direction of a slew farther down in the bottom. The movement was incredibly beautiful, at once exultant and stately, a benediction on the evening and on the river and on me. It seemed so perfectly to confirm the presence of a free nonhuman joy in the world—a joy I feel a great need to believe in— that I had the skeptic's impulse to doubt that I had seen it. If I had, I thought, it would be a sign of the presence of something heavenly in the earth. And then, one evening a year later, I saw it again.

WENDELL BERRY, *The Long-Legged House*

HALF A DOUBLE SONNET

for Ben

Their ordeal over, now the only trouble
was conveying somehow to a boy of three
that for a week or two he'd be seeing double.
Surely he wouldn't recall the surgery
years later, but what about the psychic scars?
And so, when the patch came off, they bought the toy
he'd wanted most. He held it high. "Two cars!"
he cried; and drove himself from joy to joy.
Two baby sisters . . . One was enough of Clare,
but who could complain?—considering that another
woman had stepped forward to take care
of the girls, which left him all alone with Mother.
Victory! Even when he went to pee,
he was seconded in his virility.

MARY JO SALTER

WARNING

Lovers of hunting,
and beginners seeking your prey:
Don't aim your rifles
at my happiness,
which isn't worth
the price of the bullet
(you'd waste on it).
What seems to you
so nimble and fine,
like a fawn,
and flees
every which way,
like a partridge,
isn't happiness.
Trust me:
my happiness bears
no relation to happiness.

TAHA MUHAMMAD ALI
(TRANSLATED FROM THE ARABIC
BY PETER COLE, YAHYA HIJAZI, AND GABRIEL LEVIN)

DIRECTIVE

Back out of all this now too much for us,
Back in a time made simple by the loss
Of detail, burned, dissolved, and broken off
Like graveyard marble sculpture in the weather,
There is a house that is no more a house
Upon a farm that is no more a farm
And in a town that is no more a town.
The road there, if you'll let a guide direct you
Who only has at heart your getting lost,
May seem as if it should have been a quarry—
Great monolithic knees the former town
Long since gave up pretense of keeping covered.
And there's a story in a book about it:
Besides the wear of iron wagon wheels
The ledges show lines ruled southeast-northwest,
The chisel work of an enormous Glacier
That braced his feet against the Arctic Pole.
You must not mind a certain coolness from him
Still said to haunt this side of Panther Mountain.
Nor need you mind the serial ordeal
Of being watched from forty cellar holes
As if by eye pairs out of forty firkins.
As for the woods' excitement over you
That sends light rustle rushes to their leaves,
Charge that to upstart inexperience.
Where were they all not twenty years ago?
They think too much of having shaded out
A few old pecker-fretted apple trees.
Make yourself up a cheering song of how

Someone's road home from work this once was,
Who may be just ahead of you on foot
Or creaking with a buggy load of grain.
The height of the adventure is the height
Of country where two village cultures faded
Into each other. Both of them are lost.
And if you're lost enough to find yourself
By now, pull in your ladder road behind you
And put a sign up CLOSED to all but me.
Then make yourself at home. The only field
Now left's no bigger than a harness gall.
First there's the children's house of make-believe,
Some shattered dishes underneath a pine,
The playthings in the playhouse of the children.
Weep for what little things could make them glad.
Then for the house that is no more a house,
But only a belilaced cellar hole,
Now slowly closing like a dent in dough.
This was no playhouse but a house in earnest.
Your destination and your destiny's
A brook that was the water of the house,
Cold as a spring as yet so near its source,
Too lofty and original to rage.
(We know the valley streams that when aroused
Will leave their tatters hung on barb and thorn.)
I have kept hidden in the instep arch
Of an old cedar at the waterside
A broken drinking goblet like the Grail
Under a spell so the wrong ones can't find it,

So can't get saved, as Saint Mark says they mustn't.
(I stole the goblet from the children's playhouse.)
Here are your waters and your watering place.
Drink and be whole again beyond confusion.

ROBERT FROST

OLD PEWTER

Not the age of silver, more a slither
of illiteracy under rafters:
a dented hand-me-down old smoky plate
full of blizzards, sullied and temperate.

I love unshowy pewter, my soft option
when it comes to the metals—next to solder
that weeps at the touch of a hot iron;
doleful and placid as a gloss-barked alder

reflected in the nebulous lid of a pool
where they thought I had drowned one winter day
a stone's throw from the house, when the whole
country was mist and I hid deliberately.

Glimmerings are what the soul's composed of.
Fogged-up challenges, far conscience-glitters
and hang-dog, half-truth earnests of true love.
And a whole late-flooding thaw of ancestors.

SEAMUS HEANEY

In Sunday school, I learned to think of God as a very old white-bearded man on a throne, who stood above creation and occasionally stirred it with a stick. When I am dreaming quantum dreams, what I see is an infinite web of relationship, flung across the vastness of space like a luminous net. It is made of energy, not thread. As I look, I can see light moving through it as a pulse moves through veins. What I see "out there" is no different from what I feel inside. There is a living hum that might be coming from my neurons but might just as well be coming from the furnace of the stars. When I look up at them there is a small commotion in my bones, as the ashes of dead stars that house my marrow rise up like metal filings toward the magnet of their living kin.

BARBARA BROWN TAYLOR, *The Luminous Web*

There is another world, the poet Paul Eluard famously wrote, *but it is inside this one.* And quite literally so. Certain bacteria live hundreds of meters within the earth's crust, feeding on dissolved gases and minerals rendered by the reaction of groundwater and rock. These bacteria, chemolithotrophs, have no need for solar energy. Some scientists estimate that the underground biomass, the world inside this one, might be more than double the living mass at the surface of our planet.

Perhaps we can understand now what the nineteenth-century German naturalist Alexander von Humboldt meant when he spoke of "the all-animatedness of the earth."

FORREST GANDER, *A Faithful Existence*

WELL WATER

What a girl called "the dailiness of life"
(Adding an errand to your errand. Saying,
"Since you're up . . ." Making you a means to
A means to a means to) is well water
Pumped from an old well at the bottom of the world.
The pump you pump the water from is rusty
And hard to move and absurd, a squirrel-wheel
A sick squirrel turns slowly, through the sunny
Inexorable hours. And yet sometimes
The wheel turns of its own weight, the rusty
Pump pumps over your sweating face the clear
Water, cold, so cold! you cup your hands
And gulp from the dailiness of life.

RANDALL JARRELL

The world without the sacred is not just disenchanted but deprived of some kind of depth—that is, of the sense that what we encounter is already part of a complex of interrelation before it is part of our world of perception.

ROWAN WILLIAMS, Dostoevsky

HERE

Here I am in the garden laughing
an old woman with sagging breasts
and a nicely mapped face

how did this happen
well that's who I wanted to be

at last   a woman
in the old style   sitting
stout thighs apart under
a big skirt   grandchild sliding
on   off my lap   a pleasant
summer perspiration

that's my old man across the yard
he's talking to the meter reader
he's telling him the world's sad story
how electricity is oil or uranium
and so forth   I tell my grandson
run over to your grandpa   ask him
to sit beside me for a minute   I
am suddenly exhausted by my desire
to kiss his sweet explaining lips

GRACE PALEY

I don't think in terms of being an atheist or not. I would just say that we live in mystery, and the making of this world is simply great and mysterious. I was listening, just this morning, to a man talking about finding rocks that were four billion years old. So we live in mystery. I'm not unsatisfied with that. I don't have to find a god or not a god. There's a quote—I don't remember who said it—"Find me a god because I am full of prayers." I think my husband could be described this way. He's an old Episcopalian boy. He has lost his god, but I think he's full of prayers. I'm not full of prayers. I'm full of language.

GRACE PALEY, "INCHES OF PROGRESS"

JOY

Though joy is better than sorrow joy is not great;
Peace is great, strength is great.
Not for joy the stars burn, not for joy the vulture
Spreads her gray sails on the air
Over the mountain; not for joy the worn mountain
Stands, while years like water
Trench his long sides. "I am neither mountain nor bird
Nor star; and I seek joy."
The weakness of your breed: yet at length quietness
Will cover those wistful eyes.

ROBINSON JEFFERS

WHAT ARE YEARS

What is our innocence,
what is our guilt? All are
        naked, none is safe. And whence
is courage: the unanswered question,
the resolute doubt,—
dumbly calling, deafly listening—that
in misfortune, even death,
        encourages others
        and in its defeat, stirs

the soul to be strong? He
sees deep and is glad, who
        accedes to mortality
and in his imprisonment rises
upon himself as
the sea in a chasm, struggling to be
free and unable to be,
        in its surrendering
        finds its continuing.

So he who strongly feels,
behaves. The very bird,
        grown taller as he sings, steels
his form straight up. Though he is captive,
his mighty singing
says, satisfaction is a lowly
thing, how pure a thing is joy.
        This is mortality,
        this is eternity.

MARIANNE MOORE

YES

It's like a tap-dance
Or a new pink dress,
A shit-naive feeling
Saying Yes.

Some say Good morning
Some say God bless—
Some say Possibly
Some say Yes.

Some say Never
Some say Unless
It's stupid and lovely
To rush into Yes.

What can it mean?
It's just like life,
One thing to you
One to your wife.

Some go local
Some go express
Some can't wait
To answer Yes.

Some complain
Of strain and stress
The answer may be
No for Yes.

Some like failure
Some like success
Some like Yes Yes
Yes Yes Yes.

Open your eyes,
Dream but don't guess.
Your biggest surprise
Comes after Yes.

MURIEL RUKEYSER

Right now I am thinking of something unlikely that I saw a few days ago, the morning after my town had experienced a major winter flood. In the middle of a residential street, a cast iron manhole cover was dancing in its iron collar, driven up three or four inches by such an excess of underground water that it balanced above the street, tipping and bobbing like a flower, producing an occasional bell-like chime as it touched against the metal ring. This has much to say about poetry.

For I do not want to suggest in any way that this aquifer under poetry is something silly or undangerous; it is great and a causer of every sort of damage. And I do not want to say either that the poem that prompts me to laughter is silly or light; no, it can be as heavy as a manhole cover, but it is forced up. You can see it would take an exquisite set of circumstances to ever get this right.

KAY RYAN, "A CONSIDERATION OF POETRY"

IDEAL AUDIENCE

Not scattered legions,
not a dozen from
a single region
for whom accent
matters, not a seven-
member coven,
not five shirttail
cousins; just
one free citizen—
maybe not alive
now even—who
will know with
exquisite gloom
that only we two
ever found this room.

KAY RYAN

Which is to say I am a mystic—but by memory only. For an instant, about ten years ago, I *felt* the perspective from space to earth. Sick as I may have been, I was *there*. By the use of the intelligence, of course, you can work up such perspectives at will, but it's a very different thing from *being* there—in the mixture of joy and of a sort of mad sorrow at the lot of man. What I seemed to see has remained literally the weight of the world. All the good realists, materialists and rationalists I've been able to get my hands on have done nothing to that experience. Perhaps only an equally powerful experience, certainly stronger than intellectual conviction, in another direction can ever move me.

A. R. AMMONS, *An Image for Longing*

THE CITY LIMITS

When you consider the radiance, that it does not withhold
itself but pours its abundance without selection into every
nook and cranny not overhung or hidden; when you consider

that bird's bones make no awful noise against the light but
lie low in the light as in a high testimony; when you consider
the radiance, that it will look into the guiltiest

swervings of the weaving heart and bear itself upon them,
not flinching into disguise or darkening; when you consider
the abundance of such resource as illuminates the glow-blue

bodies and gold-skeined wings of flies swarming the dumped
guts of a natural slaughter or the coil of shit and in no
way winces from its storms of generosity; when you consider

that air or vacuum, snow or shale, squid or wolf, rose or lichen,
each is accepted into as much light as it will take, then
the heart moves roomier, the man stands and looks about, the

leaf does not increase itself above the grass, and the dark
work of the deepest cells is of a tune with May bushes
and fear lit by the breadth of such calmly turns to praise.

A. R. AMMONS

Joy—it's not just a gift. In a sense it's also a duty, a task to fulfill.
Courage.

ANNA KAMIENSKA, Astonishments

AN OLD CRACKED TUNE

My name is Solomon Levi,
the desert is my home,
my mother's breast was thorny,
and father I had none.

The sands whispered, *Be separate,*
the stones taught me, *Be hard.*
I dance, for the joy of surviving,
on the edge of the road.

STANLEY KUNITZ

ACKNOWLEDGMENTS

I am grateful to Miroslav Volf, who had the idea for this book, and to the Yale Center for Faith and Culture, whose financial support made the project possible.

I have been helped at every stage by Brendan Dempsey, whose taste, intelligence, and persistence have been indispensable.

For help at crucial moments, a thanks to Bailey Pickens and Abigail Storch.

To all the people at Yale University Press, and especially to my editor Jennifer Banks, I am so grateful for the enthusiasm with which you have welcomed this project, and for the care with which you have guided it into existence.

"Still Wilderness" first appeared in *The American Scholar,* and I thank the editors for their continued support of my work.

It seems odd to dedicate an anthology of other people's poetry to particular people in my own life, but it seems odder to publish a book on joy without acknowledging my wife and daughters, without whom I wouldn't even know what the word means.